William Edward Simonds

Sir Thomas Wyatt and His Poems

William Edward Simonds

Sir Thomas Wyatt and His Poems

ISBN/EAN: 9783744710305

Printed in Europe, USA, Canada, Australia, Japan

Cover: Foto ©Thomas Meinert / pixelio.de

More available books at **www.hansebooks.com**

SIR THOMAS WYATT

AND

HIS POEMS.

Presented to the Philosophical Faculty

OF THE

KAISER WILHELM'S UNIVERSITY AT STRASSBURG FOR
THE ACQUISITION OF THE DEGREE OF DOCTOR
OF PHILOSOPHY

BY

WILLIAM EDWARD SIMONDS,

INSTRUCTOR IN GERMAN, CORNELL UNIVERSITY.

BOSTON:
D. C. HEATH AND COMPANY.
1889.

𝔘𝔫𝔦𝔟𝔢𝔯𝔰𝔦𝔱𝔶 𝔓𝔯𝔢𝔰𝔰:
JOHN WILSON AND SON, CAMBRIDGE, U.S.A.

INTRODUCTION.

IN presenting the following Essay to the attention of those for whom its subject may possess some interest, a word of explanation regarding its character and scope may not be superfluous.

As at first intended, there would have been four divisions in the Essay, subordinate and introductory to a concluding part, which should have formed the main chapter of the thesis. These four sections were to have treated of the *life* of Wyatt, the *texts*, the *metre*, and the *interpretation* of the poems. The results herein obtained were then to be brought together in the concluding portion, and applied to the accomplishment of the object sought, — an attempted chronology of the poet's works.

As the work progressed, the preliminary chapter on the life of Wyatt increased in its proportions, by reason of the material recently made available, until its subordinate character has been lost, and it now vies in importance with the section it precedes. The discussion of the metre has been omitted, lest it might detract somewhat from the unity of the plan as at last adopted in its modified form. This division of the subject may best be treated in a separate essay. The section on the texts has been made as short as possible; the purpose being to give such information merely as shall be necessary to an understanding of their condition and relation. Some results of importance in the prosecution of the work are there indicated. It is to be regretted that the original MSS. have not been available for study; without a critical examination of the MS. texts a thorough handling of the subject is impossible. The second division of the Essay aims to give an interpretation of the poems, — to determine whether or not the individual poems are so intimately related as to admit of arrangement in characteristic groups, and whether a line of order and of progress binds these groups logically together. If such an order is discoverable, it remains to reconcile the suggestions of the poems with the facts, as known, in Wyatt's life; this accomplished, it is easy to set limits chronologically to the various groups, and a chronological order, so far as practicable, will be established.

It will be obvious, therefore, that of the two divisions which now compose the Essay, neither is subordinate, each contributing to the purpose of the other; Part First, on the life of the poet, seeking a supplement in the portion devoted to his works, a logical introduction to which it aims to furnish.

No one can be more sensibly aware than is the writer

himself of the difficulties and uncertainties that characterize the attempted solution of a problem like that advanced in the pages following. The subject is one of considerable interest historically, as well as to the student of English literature in the particular epoch concerned. The work herewith introduced is in the truest sense an *essay*, and will attain its modest purpose if by its statements or suggestions it throws any light upon the career of a man whose life and works seem charged with the romantic spirit of a romantic time; if it shall aid in penetrating the obscurity that has wrapped the poet's life; or, possibly, tend to animate a collection of dry poems with the interest and personality of their author's passion.

It remains for the essayist to give expression to his appreciation of the counsel and assistance so kindly extended by his friends and teachers. Grateful recognition is due the services rendered by his fellow-students, Prof. Frank R. Butler, of the Woman's College, Baltimore, and Prof. Bliss Perry, of Williams College, on whose kindly sympathy and aid he has always been able to rely.

It would be impossible fittingly to express the obligation and the gratitude the writer feels as he recalls the encouragement and help afforded by his honored instructor, Prof. Dr. Bernhard Ten Brink, of the Strassburg University. It was by his suggestion that the Essay was undertaken, and it is largely to his care-

ful criticism and most valuable assistance that whatever merit it contains is due. ‧ It must be added also
that as the work has been completed and revised since
it last fell under Prof. Ten Brink's eye, it would be
unjust to claim his indiscriminate approval of all the
theories therein advanced; he is not responsible for the
writer's views.

CONTENTS.

Part First.

BIOGRAPHY.

SIR THOMAS WYATT

AND HIS POEMS.

Part First.

BIOGRAPHY.

SIR THOMAS WYATT, the poet, was descended from an ancient and honorable family, originally of Yorkshire, where down to the time of Henry VII. the Wyatts seem to have resided. Sir Henry Wyatt (1460–1538), the father of the poet, had borne a part in the exciting events which terminated the long struggle between the rival Houses of York and Lancaster. An adherent of the Lancastrian party, he suffered imprisonment at the hands of the usurper, Richard III., and according to a statement in the famous letter of Sir Thomas Wyatt to his son, was threatened with the rack or actually tortured in the tyrant's presence.[1] With the accession of Henry VII., in 1485, Sir Henry's star began to rise. He early became a member of the Privy Council, and one of the most trusted and esteemed of the king's advisers. He was named one of the executors of the king's will, and at the death of Henry was nominated by the Countess of Richmond to be one of the council for the management of public affairs until the young king should be able to transact business of State for himself.[2]

[1] This preserved him in prison from the hands of the tyrant that could find in his heart to see him racked. — *Wyatt's Letter to his Son.* Nott, p. 269; Aldine ed., p. lv.

[2] Herbert's Henry VIII., p. 2.

At the accession of Henry VIII. Wyatt was already living in Kent, having about the year 1493 purchased the castle and estate of Allington, near Maidstone, which remained so long as retained by them the chief residence of the family.[1] Sir Henry continued in the enjoyment of his sovereign's favor. Created Knight of the Bath at the coronation of the young king, in 1509, he was made knight-banneret on the field after the Battle of Spurs, in August, 1513. During the same year he was appointed treasurer of the king's jewels, with a salary of £50.[2] He was still a member of the Privy Council, and was constantly employed in positions of trust and honor by the king, who retained him as long as possible near his person. In 1519 he had accompanied Henry to Calais, and in capacity of knight-marshal attended his sovereign at the notable interview with Francis I. upon the Field of the Cloth of Gold.[3] In 1527 he had the honor of entertaining Henry at the Castle of Allington,[4] and in 1533 we find him holding the honorable position of ewerer to the king.[5] It has been stated by one or two writers that Sir Henry held the office of Treasurer of the Royal Chamber during the period 1525–28.[6] The truth is that he was appointed to this office at least two years before the date assigned; this is abundantly proved by the State Papers now accessible. The earliest paper bearing his name and title is an indenture of date 18 February, 1523, in which occurs the name of "Sir Henry Wyat, treasurer of the Chamber."[7] Again, under date of 24 February, 1523, is a memorandum that by the cardinal's (Wolsey)

---

[1] Hasted's Kent, ii. 184.
[2] Calendar of State Papers, Henry VIII. i. 4125. For Sir Henry Wyatt, the king's councillor. To be treasurer of the king's jewels; with annuity of £50, and appointment of two yeomen and one page. *Delivered* Westm. 26, May 5, Hen. VIII.
[3] Calendar of State Papers, iii. 241, 243.
[4] Cavendish's History of Cardinal Wolsey, ch. xiii.
[5] Calendar of State Papers, vi. 601, 701.
[6] Ald. ed., p. x; Riverside ed., p. xii.
[7] Calendar of State Papers, iii. 2835.

warrant, dated 24 February, 14 Hen. VIII., Thos. Magnus received from Sir Henry Wyatt for the army on the Scotch border, and to be issued for necessaries by command of the Earl of Surrey, £20,000.[1] Unfortunately the patent granting the office to Sir Henry Wyatt does not appear to be extant.

Sir Henry Wyatt died at Allington in 1531. His character and life are eloquently set forth by his son, Sir Thomas, in the latter's first letter to his own son, Thomas Wyatt the younger. This tribute to the excellences of his father's character must have been written almost immediately after Sir Henry's decease, as Sir Thomas was at the time in Spain, whence he returned to England in 1539. By his wife Anne, daughter of John Skinner, of Reigate in Surrey,[2] Sir Henry Wyatt left three children, — a daughter, Margaret, who married Sir Anthony Lee ; and two sons, Thomas and Henry. Of these, the younger brother, Henry, lived the life of a retired gentleman of means, presumably in Kent ;[3] while the elder, Thomas, is known to us not only as a successful courtier and diplomat, but even better as a poet of no mean fame, in connection with his friend Henry Howard, Earl of Surrey, reputed for one of " the two chief lanternes of light to all others that have since employed their pennes upon English Poesie."[4]

Thomas Wyatt the poet was born at Allington Castle in the year 1503. He was entered as student at St. John's College at Cambridge in 1515, where, three years later, he took his degree of B. A., and his Master's degree in 1520.

It was customary then for young men of rank to spend some time at Paris immediately after leaving the university ; and therefore it has been a matter of conjecture whether or no the poet visited France at this time. No record of such visit, however, has as yet been discovered, and it is still uncertain whether

---

[1] Calendar of State Papers, iii. 2852. Compare also Nos. 2876, 2956, 3023, 3177, 3282, 3375, 3542, 3597, 3650.

[2] Collins's Peerage, iii. 428.   [3] Heralds' College, Essex, c. 21, 1634.

[4] Puttenham's Arte of English Poesie (Arber's ed) p. 76.

Wyatt caught his first glimpse of Continental life at this or a later period. It is certain that Wyatt's marriage must have taken place about this time ; *i. e.*, in 1520 or 1521, when he was about eighteen years of age. This fact we learn from the inquisition made immediately after the poet's death, in October, 1542, wherein his son Thomas is referred to as being "of the age of twenty-one years and upwards," which would place his birth in the year 1521.[1] The lady whom Wyatt married was Elizabeth, daughter of Thomas Brooke, Lord Cobham.

Wyatt now entered upon his career of success. The esteem in which his father was held at Court would naturally have served him as a passport to the good-will of his sovereign, and the young man's own endowments, both of mind and body, were of a nature to make him popular with his associates, and to win the friendship of the king. Wyatt soon became prominent among Henry's courtiers, and noted as a man of influence at Court, enjoying the royal favor in an unusual degree.

Very little of actual record has come down to us respecting the poet's life at this period. It has been taken for granted that he was engaged either in attendance at the Court or in serving with the army as a volunteer. The supposition is that much of his leisure time was devoted to literary pursuits and to the usual employments of a gentleman of his talents and position. Edward Hall, the chronicler of Henry's reign, describes a feat of arms performed before the king at Greenwich on Christmas Day of 1525, and says that Thomas Wyatt, then an esquire of the royal household, was one of the fourteen challengers on that occasion.[2] In 1527, as is well known, the young courtier joined the company of Sir John Russell, special ambassador to Rome, and with that nobleman travelled to some extent in Italy. A record, likewise familiar, has come down to us from the year 1533, which mentions the service performed

---

[1] Nott, p. lxxiv.
[2] A description of this feat of arms is given by Dr. Nott in the prefatory memoir, p. ix.

by Thomas Wyatt, in place of his father, Sir Henry, at the royal banquet given in honor of the coronation of Anne Boleyn. With the exception of these three incidents, Wyatt's biographers have thrown no light hitherto on the circumstances of the poet's life until the advent of the year 1536. Happily the publication of recent volumes in the series of "Calendars of State Papers," issued under the direction of the Master of the Rolls, has made us acquainted with certain other records heretofore inaccessible, and has brought to light a few additional facts in the life of the poet-statesman which add quite materially to the rather scant biography we have until now possessed.

The earliest mention of the poet's name occurs with no further comment in a list of names of persons comprising the royal household for the year 1516. Sir Henry Wyatt was a member of the household as Knight of the Body ; and Sir Henry's thirteen-year old son was at that time learning to serve his royal master in the character of page. Both facts are attested by the list, the name of "Th. Wyet" being placed among those of the "Sewers Extraordinary" to the king.[1]

From a paper early in the series, but removed by several years from the record above cited, we learn that Sir Henry Wyatt, in his capacity of Treasurer of the Chamber, was employed in collecting and disbursing moneys destined for use in the war with France. It was in connection with one of those forced loans or subsidies demanded by Henry's minister which brought such a storm of popular indignation about the cardinal's head. But this record of accounts is of interest to us solely from the fact that we find the name of Thomas Wyatt mentioned in connection with the performance of his father's duties. On several occasions it became necessary to forward money "for the king's affairs in the North," requiring to be delivered at the Abbey of St. Mary's in York. Twice was the conveyance and delivery of this money intrusted to young Wyatt, — once in October, and again in November of the year

[1] Calendar of State Papers, ii. 2735.

1523. The sum in each case amounted to £2000.[1] In addition to the entry in Sir Henry's own account, we find later on a release to the Abbot of St. Mary's, in which reference is made to both sums received by hand of Thomas Wyatt.[2] If for no other reason, these entries are of interest as at least fixing the presence of Wyatt in England, and affording a hint, if no more, as to his employment at this time.

In March of the year 1526 Henry VIII. despatched a special ambassador to the King of France to felicitate the latter upon his escape from the hands of the Emperor Charles V. and his return to his own realm. This ambassador was Sir Thomas Cheney, a member of the Privy Council.[3] He arrived at Bordeaux on the 6th of April;[4] and among the gentlemen of his suite was Thomas Wyatt. In May we find the Court at Cognac; here it became necessary to transmit a message of special importance to the king, and Wyatt was selected by the ambassador to fulfil this duty; he was also charged to inform Henry

---

[1] Calendar of State Papers, iv. 214. Loan for the war with France. (Account of Sir Henry Wyat, treasurer of the Chamber, of the money paid to him by the collectors of divers shires. 14 Henry VIII.) Among the "Payments of the Loan money made by Wiat," 1 July to 1 April, 15 Henry VIII.

Sent by Thos. Wiatt, to be conveyed to St. Mary's Abbey, York, for the king's affairs in the North, 26 October, £2000, and 20 November, £2000, his costs £17 1s.

[2] Ibid., 2322. The Subsidy. Release to Edm. Whalley, Abbot of St. Mary, York, receiver of the subsidy in the province of York, of the following sums received by him: £20,000 of Sir Hen. Wyat, treasurer of the king's chamber, by the hand of Thos. Draper; £2000 from the same by Thos. Wyet, Esq.; another £2000 from and by the same. Del. Westm. 16 July, 18 Hen. VIII.

[3] Ibid., iv. 2037, Wolsey to Francis I. The king is rejoiced at Francis's return to his realm. Sends Sir Thos. Cheyney to reside as ambassador with Dr. Tailleur. Desires credence for him. (Wolsey writes to the same effect to Robertet, under date — Westm., 20 March, 1526.)

[4] Ibid., 2075. Sir Thos. Cheyne to Wolsey. "Arrived here between 7 and 8 A. M. yesterday." Bordeaux, 7 April, 1526.

more at length of men and manners as he had observed them at the Court of France. The letter signed by the envoy and by the resident ambassador closes with a most complimentary reference to the young man's sagacity and talent, — the earliest comment we possess upon the characteristic qualities of the future diplomat.[1] That the Wyatt here referred to is not Sir Henry, as Mr. Brewer deems, but his son Thomas, is hardly to be doubted. Confirmatory evidence is at hand in a note of Wolsey's to the king, in which he speaks of the arrival of this message from the ambassadors, and refers to despatches for "young Wyat," who returns therewith to France.[2] Sir Henry was now full five and sixty years of age ; it is incredible that he be the person meant ; and we know nothing of the existence of any other Wyatt at this time busy in affairs of Court. The fact seems to be that the young courtier was serving what was perhaps a recognized apprenticeship in the art of diplomacy. It was the custom then, as it has been since, for young men of rank and promise to be employed in just such service, that they might acquire a practical experience in diplomatic methods, and thus become qualified to discharge important missions under credentials of their own. The last allusion among the papers to Wyatt's present visit is under date of 21 May, when Cheney, writing to Henry, describes an interview with Francis and says :

"We told him the gentleman had returned who had been dispatched to England. He said he would be joyous to hear from your Highness, his most dear and loving brother. Presented Wyatt, who with good and discreet behaviour declared the same according[ly]."[3]

[1] Calendar of State Papers, 2135. Cheyne and Tayler to Wolsey. "Send the bearer Wyatt, who can show your Grace of a part of the commodities belonging to this house, and in likewise of the n[ames] and countenance of the noblemen and gentlemen hereunto . . . daily; for he hath been at the Court with us from time to [time], and as we think, hath as much wit to mark and remember every thing he saith as any young man hath in England." Cognac, 1 May, 1526.

[2] Ibid., iv., 2163.   [3] Ibid., 2194.

2

Cheney was recalled that same month; and as no further mention is made of Wyatt's name, we presume he returned to England in the ambassador's company.

It was just about one year subsequent to this that Wyatt accompanied Sir John Russell on his embassy to the Pope. The fact is now authenticated, and the circumstances, so far as known, are so familiar as to call for no extended reference here. In a letter written from Rome under date 11 February, 1527, Russell writes to Wolsey of their arrival thus : —

" I, Russell, arrived at Civita Vecchia on the 4th. Remained a day and a half before I could get horses, although Andrea Doreo did what he could, and accompanied me with certain foot and hand guns. We arrived here the second day after our departure thence, and the Pope sent me a Turkey horse on which he rides himself, with another for Mr. Wyatt, and good horses for my company." [1]

One incident of this journey deserves more prominence than has hitherto been accorded it. Sir John Russell, it appears, about setting forth from Rome on his way to Venice, met with some slight accident, — a fall from his horse, or something of the kind, — which was serious enough to hinder his proceeding; so while the ambassador remained at Narni, Wyatt was despatched to Venice, where he arrived safely, and, with the letters, waited on the Venetian Council. [2] This duty done, the young Englishman, desirous of seeing the country, and " pretending soon to come by Bologna and Florence " to Rome, made a pleasure-trip to Ferrara. His excursion ended, however, rather disastrously in his capture by Spanish troops of the emperor, who, in spite of Wyatt's safe-conduct from the Duke of Ferrara, demanded a ransom of three thousand ducats. The affair proved serious ; and a tedious course of negotiation

---

[1] Calendar of State Papers, iv. 2875.

[2] Ibid., iv. 2931. Russell, having met with an accident, remains at Narni and sends Wyatt with his letters to Sir Gregory Casale at Venice, who goes with Wyatt to the Venetian Council. (Letter from Casale dated March 2, 1527.)

seemed inevitable, when the matter was somewhat prematurely settled by the sudden appearance of the prisoner at Bologna, where he seems to have arrived when least expected.[1] It is not quite clear whether Wyatt escaped, or owed his release to the efforts of his friends.[2] From the tone of the letters written by Russell and Casale reporting the incident to Wolsey, it may be gathered that the ambassadors were a trifle exercised at Wyatt's escapade ; the two letters which are appended form quite a contrast to Cheney's letter, written from France the year before, so commendatory in its reference to Wyatt's wit and bearing. Although no blame attaches itself to the young attaché because of this incident in the Italian journey, its occurrence may nevertheless illustrate a certain daring, a heedlessness of consequences, which seems to have.marked his character at this time, and which occasionally betrayed him into situations of unjustifiable exposure. The party remained in Italy until about the first of May, when they returned to England.

The next fact of importance noted occurs under date of the following year ; but before proceeding to consider that, it is necessary to discuss another matter which here finds its appropriate place. It has been recently suggested upon dubious authority that Thomas Wyatt succeeded his father in the office of treasurer of the Chamber. The assertion appears to have been first made by Mr. John Payne Collier, in his edition of the

[1] Calendar of State Papers, iv. 3011. Russell and Casale to Wolsey. Wyatt went to Venice after Russell's hurt, then to Ferrara, being desirous of seeing the country, " pretending soon to come by Bologna and Florence hither." Notwithstanding the Duke's safe-conduct, he was taken by the Spaniards. They demanded three thousand ducats for his ransom, notwithstanding Russell's protestations. He has since managed to escape. Rome, April 1, 1527.

[2] The uncertainty is due to the existence of the following : —
Calendar, iv. 3023. John Casale, prothonotary to Wolsey. The troops who were collecting necessaries at Ferrara have been sent for, as he will see by the enclosed letter of a servant of his, whom he had sent thither to obtain the liberation of Wyatt, which he has at last effected. April 6, 1527.

Trevelyan Papers, where he calls attention to a certain entry
in which former incumbents of this office are named in order;
in this list Sir Thomas Wyatt's name immediately precedes that
of Sir Brian Tuke. In a foot-note, Collier draws attention to
the entry, and announces the discovery of the supposed fact
that Sir Thomas had thus succeeded his father as treasurer.[1] It
is a singular coincidence that in the State Papers Calendar,
iv. 3104, under date of May 7, 1527, is a record of payments
made " by Sir Henry Gwildeforde, knight, and Sir Thomas Wyat,
knight, in building a banketing house at the King his manor of
Greenwich." To this entry Brewer adds a parenthesis : " In a
later hand." Following immediately upon this the same account
enumerates sums of money received by Sir Henry Guildeforde
" and of Sir Henry Wiat, treasurer of the Chamber." The coincidence lies in the fact that this entry " in a later hand " occurs
at just the date to substantiate Mr. Collier's theory ; Sir Brian
Tuke having been appointed treasurer in 1528. This mention
of " Sir Thomas Wyat " is of course an error, and is noted as
such by the editor of the Calendar in the Notes and Errata,
p. 3535. During the year 1527, the period in question, we find
several entries proving conclusively that Sir Henry retained the
office down to April, 1528, when Sir Brian Tuke was appointed
to succeed him.[2] Having thus disposed of a bit of false biography, we now come to the notice of a fact which helps to throw
considerable light upon a period in the poet's life long involved
in obscurity.

[1] Trevelyan Papers, part ii. ; Sir William Cavendishe's Book, p. 12.
[2] Calendar of State Papers, iv. 3121. Receipt by Raphael Maruffus of
a certain sum of money " by the hands of Sir Henry Wyatt, treasurer."
May 15, 1527.
Ibid., 3380. The Earl of Northumberland's Accounts. 10, ii. For a
loan to the king paid to Sir Harry Wyatt, £100.
Ibid., 3739. Wm. Kebyll. Order from Sir Henry Wyat to John Jen-
yns for the payment of fifty . . . to Wm Kebyll, towards making New
Year's gifts.
Ibid., 4170. Brian Tuke. To be treasurer of the Chamber *vice* Sir
Henry Wyat. *Del.* Hampton Court, 13 April, 19 Hen. VIII.

Among the papers which the Calendar now brings into notice we find an account of salaries paid to the different officers at Calais for the year 1528; and in this account there is a list of the various officials comprising the Council of Calais for that year. One of the names enumerated is that of Thos. Wyott, Esq., high marshal, with a command of sixteen men.[1]

In September he is still there, and receives a license to import Gascony wine and Toulouse wood.[2] In June, 1530, he receives a second grant "To be marshal of the town," etc., of Calais.[3] No copy of the original grant has as yet been found among the papers. In November, 1530, Sir Edward Ryngely is appointed "marshal of the town and marches of Calais . . . *vice* Thomas Wyat, squire of the Body."[4] There can be no question here as to identity. Contemporary writers refer to Wyatt's military service,[5] and it has always been supposed that

---

[1] Calendar of State Papers, iv. 5102 (2). An account of the salaries of the different officers at Calais, with an estimate of the charge for one year. I. The Council : Sir Robt. Wyngfeld, deputy . . . Thos. Wyott, Esq., high marshal, at 2s. a day, and 20 marks in reward by year; 5 men under him, each at 8d. a day, and 11 at 6d. a day.

[2] Ibid., iv. 5978. Grants in September, 1529 (26). Thos. Wyat, squire of the Body, and marshal of Calais. License to import 1000 tuns of Gascoigne wine or Tolles (Toulouse) woad. *Del.* le More, 26 Sept. 21 Hen. VIII.

[3] Ibid., iv. 6490. Grants in June, 1530 (23). Thos Wyat, squire of the Body. To be marshal of the town, etc., of Calais, with the same number of soldiers as Sir John Wallop or Sir Edward Guldeforde or any other marshal of the said town and marches had and with the same fees. Windsor Castle, 11 June, 22 Hen. VIII. *Del.* Westm., 3 June.

[4] Ibid., iv. 6751. Grants in November, 1530 (24). Sir Edward Ryngeley. To be marshal of the town and marches of Calais; to hold the said office in like manner as John Wallop and Edward Guldeford held the same, *vice* Thos. Wyat, squire of the Body. York Place, 22 Nov., 22 Hen. VIII. *Del.* Westm , 24 Nov.

[5] Leland, Nænia, v. 52.

> " Inter Cœlicolas nuper certamen obortum;
> Dissidii vero causa Viatus erat.
> Mars ait; 'Est noster juvenum fortissimus ille.'
> Phœbus at, 'Ingenii flos' ait 'ille meus.' "

it was at this period that such service was performed. If confirmatory evidence were required, it would be found in the record of a grant in May of 1530, by which John Williams is appointed to the office of clerk of the king's jewels, which office was granted by patent, October 21, 1524, to "Thomas Wyat, esquire of the Royal Body, son and heir of [Sir] Henry Wyat."[1] It is most unlikely that there were two Thomas Wyatts at one time esquires of the Body; and as the Thomas Wyatt, marshal of Calais, and the Thomas, son of Sir Henry, were each designated as esquire of the Body, it is probable that they were one and the same person; it becomes pretty clearly evident, therefore, that the marshal of Calais was the Wyatt of these memoirs. As to the exact date of Wyatt's appointment, there is uncertainty, owing to apparent confusion in the records cited. If Sir John Wallop was promoted to the lieutenancy of Calais Castle by patent of June 23, 1530, but holding the office from October 6, 1529,[2] it is probable that Wyatt, who received his grant on the same day with Wallop, entered upon his duties at about the same date as the latter, whom he succeeded on the latter's promotion. But in the grant of September, 1529, Wyatt has the title of marshal, and even as early as the end of 1528 we find his name upon the list of officers above referred to. Despite this uncertainty, it is without doubt a fact that during the greater part of the years 1529–30 Thomas Wyatt was serving the interests of the king in the somewhat responsible position of high marshal of Calais. It must not be overlooked, either, that from

[1] Calendar of State Papers, vol. iv. Notes and Errata, p. 3537, 6418. Grants in May, 1530. (8) John Wylliams. To be clerk of the king's jewels with 20 marks a year, after the death or surrender of Thomas Wyat, esquire of the Royal Body, son and heir of [Sir] Henry Wyat, who holds the office by patent 21 Oct., 16 Hen. VIII. Greenwich, 6 Apr., 22 Hen. VIII. Del. Westm., 8 May.

[2] Ibid., iv. 6490 (23). (Following first grant to Thos. Wyat.) Sir John Walop. To be lieutenant of Calais Castle from 6 Oct. last, with 49 soldiers, etc. Dated: Windsor Castle, 13 June, 22 Hen. VIII. Del. Westm., 23 June.

October, 1524, until May, 1531, Wyatt held the office of clerk of the king's jewels. We have already produced a grant under date of May, 1530, in which John Williams is appointed to succeed Wyatt on the latter's death, or on surrender of his patent. This surrender actually took place in 1531, when the real grant of the office followed.[1]

Two or three unimportant records occur during this same year.[2] Of greater importance is the notice of the appointment of Wyatt in February, 1532, to be a commissioner of the peace for Essex.[3]

This same year of 1532 was signalized by the fall of Wolsey. Dr. Nott refers to the hostility of both the Wyatts, and thinks that Thomas Wyatt contributed to the causes that brought about the cardinal's ruin.[4]

At the coronation of Queen Anne Boleyn in June of 1533, Wyatt served as representative for his father in performing the duties of ewerer to the king on the occasion of the royal banquet.[5]

[1] Calendar of State Papers, v. 278 (10). John Williams. Grant in reversion of the office of clerk of the king's jewels, with fees of 20 marks a year, which office was granted by patent 21 Oct. 16 Henry VIII. to Thomas Wiat, esquire of the Royal Body, son and heir of Henry Wyat. *Westm.*, 8 May. Pat. 23 Hen. VIII.

[2] Ibid., v. 119 (71). William Bunsall, of Bloffleming, Cornw., tanner. Pardon for having on the 8th Feb. 20 Hen. VIII., with others, robbed Thomas Wyatt at Bloffleming of certain property. York Place, 24 Feb. 22 Hen. VIII. *Del.* Westm., 27 Feb.

Ibid., 1285 (5). Cromwell's "Obligations and Bills." "Inventory of the desperat bills remaining in the custody of the said John Williams." . . . Alen Hawte (for Thos. Wyat's debt to the king).

[3] Ibid., v. 838 (13). Commissioners of the Peace. Among the names upon the list for Essex is that of "Thos. Wyott."

[4] Nott, Memoirs, xxxii.

[5] Calendar of State Papers, vi. 601. Coronation of Anne Boleyn. . . . Order and sitting at dinner. "Thos. Wiat was chief sewer for his father, Sir Henry." June 8, 1533.

Ibid., 701. Anne Boleyn's Coronation . . . Officers and noblemen with others who did service until the morrow after Midsummer Day, 25 Hen. VIII., etc. "Sir Henry Wyatt chief ewer, supplied by his son Thos. Wyatt." June 25, 1533.

Under date of May 15, 1534, a letter written by John Rokewood to Lord Lisle, who was then commandant at Calais, relates that "On Wednesday there was a great affray between
Mr. Wyatte and the sergeants of London, in which one of the
sergeants was slain. For this Mr. Wyatt is committed to the
Fleet."[1] Gairdner (the successor of Mr. Brewer in the editing
of the Calendars) indexes this letter under the name of Sir
Henry Wyatt; but Sir Henry was now in his seventy-fourth
year, and it is rather improbable that the poet's father is the
Wyatt here referred to. Sir Thomas's own son, the younger
Thomas Wyatt, was only about thirteen years of age, and probably not sufficiently precocious to become involved in an
affray of this kind, and get himself clapped into the Fleet at
that early date. There is of course the possibility that some
other person of the name is the one to whom reference is made ;
but there is no reason why we should not, on the other hand,
refer the adventure to the poet himself. It is doubtful if any
other Wyatt were in a position then to create such a disturbance ; nor is the incident out of keeping with what we suppose Wyatt's character to have been at this period, when, if
we may judge from his own self-arraignment in the first letter
to his son, a boldness in adventure and a certain amount of
heedlessness as to consequences brought him "into a thousand
dangers and hazards, enmities, hatreds, prisonments, despites,
and indignations."[2] Here undoubtedly the father, in his desire to impress a useful lesson on the boy, has been too zealous
in charging his own youth with an over-weight of folly ; still
there is presumably a degree of sincerity in the self-rebuke,
and more or less ground in reality to warrant regret and dissat-
isfaction at the recollections of earlier years. To be sure, this
famous letter was written only four years later than the occurrence of this incident in London ; but Wyatt became a changed
man within the limit of those four years, and we may look upon

[1] Calendar of State Papers, vii. 674.
[2] Letter to his son, Nott, p. 269; Ald. ed , lvi.

the events of the year 1536 as marking the turning-point in
his career. It may be well to note that this affray occurred in
the month of May; and Wyatt, in one of his later sonnets,
speaks of

"th' haps most unhappy
That me betide in May most commonly."[1]

Another ground for referring this affair to Wyatt is to be
found in the fact that the writer of this letter had been under-
marshal at Calais during the period of Wyatt's service there,
and was, it is likely, on terms of intimacy with him; hence it
was natural enough for Rokewood to report the occurrence to
Lord Lisle as a matter of special interest, perhaps to both.
No serious consequences further than a short detention seem
to have resulted from the incident. In the month following,
Wyatt received an important command in the king's army, with
license to keep twenty men in livery.[2]

In February and March of the year 1535 an interesting correspondence appears to have taken place, traces of which are
found in the form of three letters still existing among the State
Papers. This correspondence is in regard to the bestowal of
the stewardship of Westmalling Abbey, then vacant through the
death of the former incumbent. This stewardship must have
been a profitable holding; for the vacant office seems to have
been coveted by several gentlemen of note. Most prominent
among the applicants were Richard Cromwell, kinsman of
Henry's minister, and Thomas Wyatt, whose suit received the
favor and support of the king. There was, moreover, a third
claimant, Sir Edward Wotton, who, by right of a former promise made by the abbess, received, and for a short time at

---

[1] Sonnet: " Ye that in love . . ." Nott, p. 5; Ald. ed., p. 5.
[2] Calendar of State Papers, vii. 922 (17). Thomas Wiatt, esquire of
the Royal Body. Grant for life of the conduct and command of all men
able for war in the seven hundreds of co. Kent, the parishes of Ten-
derden, Gowderst, Stapleherst, and in the Isle of Oxney, Kent; with
license to have twenty men in his livery. *Del.* Westm., 23 June, 26
Hen. VIII.

least held, the office ; but fearful of bringing down upon his own
head the displeasure of the minister, he seems to have surren-
dered his patent and to have joined the rest in urging Wyatt's
suit upon the abbess, Cromwell meanwhile having naturally
withdrawn that of his nephew. The abbess appears to have
been incorrigible, however, with fear of neither king nor minister before her eyes ; and as to the actual result of the matter,
the correspondence gives no light. The first letter in the series
is addressed to Thos. Wyat, Esq., by Eliz. Rede, abbess of
Malling. In it the abbess says : —

" I have received the King's letter for you to be high steward of
our house.   Half a year ago I promised it to Sir Thos. Willoughby for his son, after the death of master Fisher.   I have
also received a letter from Mr. Secretary for a kinsman of his
(Ric. Cromwell), and have informed him of my promise, and also
that if Sir Thos. Willoughby is contented to absolve me, Mr.
Secretary shall have it.   Sir Thos. Nevill has also written to me
to have the said office for himself, and I have promised that if he
can obtain the favor of master Secretary and Mr. Willoughby, he
shall have it.   If I had known the King's pleasure before, you
should have had it." Westmallyng, Feb. 20, 1535.[1]

The second letter (dated Bocton Malherbe, Saturday, Feb.
27, 1535[2]) is from Sir Edw. Wotton to Cromwell.   In this
letter Sir Edward remonstrates against Cromwell's urging him
by his letters to resign his patent of the stewardship of the
Abbey of Malling, the king having written to the abbess in
favor of Master Thomas Wyatt.   The grant he obtained under
the convent seal " was in fulfillment of a promise of the Abbess
many years past."

The third letter, likewise from Sir Edw. Wotton to Cromwell,
is of special interest, not only as throwing a side-light upon
men and manners of that day, but as revealing something of
Wyatt's position at Court, and attesting Cromwell's friendship
and the favor of the king.   It contains the following : —

---

[1] Calendar of State Papers, viii. 249.   [2] Ibid , viii. 275.

" On my return home I went to Malling to the Abbess, and declared your great displeasure towards her for her late demeanor to the King and you touching the high stewardship of her house, and that you would make shortly more plainly to appear to her. I told her I could reckon no way of help unless she would make a new patent of the office under her convent seal to Master Wyatt, and send it to you with mine, that Wyat might see it was cancelled. I offered to restore mine to her, on which she said that if I would so do she would cancel it before my face, but she would make no promise to Wyat. I told her that I only resigned on condition that she would give it to Wyat, and recover your favour, and that she must think me of very mean wit if I would relinquish my hold after this sort, — only that I saw more danger to her than commodity to myself by keeping it. Not being able to discover her determination, except that she would write to you, I left my patent with her and departed, not a little in her displeasure. She said she might have bestowed it upon others, who would ' much better have shifted therewith ' than I have done. Thus I have lost an office with the thanks of neither party. Beseeching you to continue good master to me." Bocton Malherbe, 6 March, 1535.[1]

What delicious character-painting this is ! In the background looms the iron will of Cromwell, which the politic knight is shrewd to see and dread. How expressive is that phrase : " your displeasure . . . that you would make shortly more plainly to appear to her !" And yet, with no evidence to the contrary, who knows but that this exasperating lady had her way, and baffled king, minister, and all ! Wyatt himself refers to the matter so late as June, 1537, in a way to indicate that the affair was not even then agreed upon. The reference occurs in a letter written to Cromwell just as Wyatt is on the point of embarking at Hythe on his way to Spain. He says : —

". . . I humbly recommend unto you my matter of Mallyng, in which I found at the King's hands so good inclination that I am glad of the hope that I have, which is, that it is in your hands."[2]

[1] Calendar of State Papers, viii. 349.
[2] This letter is printed in the Ald. ed., p. xxiii.

In this same letter Wyatt seems to speak as though the office were really his, declaring that the value of the holding is scarcely forty pounds a year to him; but the reference is obscure, and some other property may be meant. A search among the Decrees of the Court of Augmentations and through both sets of Conventual Leases fails to bring to light any enrolment of the deed which would presumably have been made by the abbess and convent, in case the office had been conferred upon the poet.

In July of the same year, 1535, Wyatt leased for a term of eighty years the estate in Yorkshire known as Aryngden Park.[1] The year 1536 was an important one in Wyatt's life. It was the year of the trial and execution of Anne Boleyn; it was also the year of the great revolt under Lord Darcy and Lord Hussey in the North. Above all, it was the year in which Cromwell's policy of making the king's will absolute and supreme rapidly approached consummation. When we proceed to consider the life of a public man of that day, — a man of noble family, a courtier, — it is in a measure necessary to give at least a glance to the political history of the time. The principal events of Henry's reign are tolerably familiar. The decade just completed had been signalized by the long, persistent clamoring for the king's divorce; the cruel treatment of Queen Catharine had been followed by the rise of the Boleyns and the brilliant exaltation of Henry's new favorite. The great cardinal had fallen, and the iron power of the new minister griped harder and harder every day. A certain stage in the development of Cromwell's policy was noted by the death of Bishop Fisher and of Sir Thomas More, who had just perished on the scaffold. These were among the more conspicuous events which had marked

---

[1] Calendar of State Papers, viii. 1158 (16). Thos. Wyatt. Lease for 80 years of all messuages, lands, woods, etc., in Heptonstall and Sourbye, in the parish of Halliffax, Yorks., which were in the time of Ric. duke of York, 30 Henry VI., and long before, enclosed with hedges and pales for keeping deer, and now commonly called Aryngden Park. Riding, 9 July, 27 Hen. VIII. *Del.* Westm., 11 July.

the years of the decade now closing; but aside from these ex-
ternal facts, others, perhaps more momentous, were just tran-
spiring. The rise of the new learning had been inaugurated
and advanced by men like Erasmus, Colet, and More. The
new ideas which had had their birth in the work of Luther had
been steadily permeating the English folk. Forces partly con-
cealed, but long fermenting, were approaching their development. It was this secret working in the hearts of men that was
more worthy to be, and more truly was, the germ of the English
Reformation than were the extreme ideas of an absolutist like
Cromwell, or the lust of a selfish, passionate king like Henry.

In Germany, Henry's name was held in detestation by the
Lutherans, because of the transparent shallowness of his Protes-
tantism; at home he had alienated the sympathies of the people
at large through his cruelty to Catharine and the shamelessness
of his relations with Anne Boleyn. All classes were disaffected.
During the brief period of prosperity following Anne's marriage
to the king it was hardly safe for the new queen to appear out-
side the palace-gates, so bitter was the feeling of the common
people towards her. On one occasion previous to the marriage,
she had been attacked by a mob of London women seven or
eight thousand strong, who would have killed her if they had
succeeded in the attempt to make her prisoner. This feeling
was as strong against the king as against his mistress, and was
not confined to the commons; many of Henry's nobles were
ripe for treason, and there was a spirit of sullen opposition to
the will of the king which made rebellion probable, and even
encouraged a plan of invasion from abroad which was to end
in the establishment of a foreign power upon the English throne.
Such a state of affairs called for prompt and vigorous measures,
and the measures which Cromwell chose to wield were speedily
at hand. The country was filled with spies; the gibbet gave
place only to the block. The historian Green characterizes the
years of Cromwell's administration as the one period in English
history which deserves the name given to the rule of Robespierre :

"It was the English Terror." "So vigilant" was Cromwell, as
Cranmer pleaded afterwards to the king, "so vigilant to preserve
your majesty from all treasons." Treasons there were, but it is
surprising that they were so few. It is of such a policy that treason
is bred ; but, as it was, there were more rebellious thoughts than
found expression in open action. The nobles were for the most
part too firmly united in their sovereign to break their allegiance
to him.[1]

Through all the commotion and excitement of those years
the Wyatts, father and son, retained the confidence of Henry,
and stood firm in their loyal devotion to him. That the working of the under-current was not without effect upon the younger
man, is apparent in all the productions of the years which follow ;
and it is for this reason that we have dealt thus at length with a
subject which is of great importance for understanding the development of the poet's character and work. The year 1536 was
the turning-point in Wyatt's life. He was but thirty-three years
of age ; but from now on, his writings become more and more
deeply tinged with the sober shades born of experience and
reflection. It was impossible for a mind like his, — a mind so
responsive to the charms of the new learning, — to pass through
the troubled times of which we speak without profoundly realiz-
ing the uncertainty of fortune and the vanity of human success.
He was not deaf to the utterances of the still voices of the
time ; but their commands for him did not conflict with his
duty to the king. No thought of disloyalty could occur to
him. It was —

"My King, my country, alone for whom I live,"[2]

that he sang when leaving Spain for his native land, in 1539.
He was the zealous servant of the king, and even retained the
friendship of Cromwell to the end.

[1] In connection with this section see Green's Short History of the
English People, ch. vi. sect. vi.

[2] Nott's ed., p. 71.

This change in the tone of Wyatt's poems, to which reference has been made above, was a perfectly natural one ; if it came earlier in his life, or was more marked at that age, than is usual, the reason is to be found in the impressive lessons of the day and place in which he lived.   The change was not due, as some of his biographers have argued, to the sombre thoughts and troubled conscience aroused by the pitiful end of Anne Boleyn. Regarding the relationship which had existed between the young courtier-poet and Catharine's fair maid of honor, much has been said and very little really known.   Certain allusions in the love-poems make it pretty evident that on the poet's side, at least, some real affection for the lady had existed ; as to the nature and reliability of these allusions, we shall be better able to form a judgment in that part of our essay devoted to the interpretation of the poems, which is to follow.

Wyatt's name has been connected with the record of Anne Boleyn's trial and condemnation.   It is well known that he was a prisoner in the Tower during the period of Anne's confine- ment ; he himself alludes to this imprisonment in his oration before the judges at his trial in 1541.   The precise nature of his offence is unknown ; Wyatt, in the reference just noted, says that it was a matter between himself and the Duke of Suffolk.[1] Whatever the charge, it is evident that the matter caused little anxiety to Wyatt's father, and that the poet's innocence was soon satisfactorily established.   There is a letter of Henry's, di- rected to Archdeacon Pate, then ambassador to the emperor, bearing date of April 25, 1536, and subscribed with the words "*endd by Wyat.*"[2]   If Wyatt, therefore, enjoyed the confidence of the king sufficiently to be employed by him at that date to perform the duties of a secretary, it is evident that the cause of his im- prisonment must have rested upon some evidence unexpectedly discovered, or on some outbreak of sudden passion at a later provocation.

[1] Wyatt's Defence : Nott, p. 299 ; Ald. ed., p. lxxxvi.
[2] Calendar of State Papers, x. 726.

Upon the 7th of May Sir Henry sent a letter to his son, in which reference is made to the treason with which George Boleyn, Norris, Weston, and the others were accused, and urges his son to give the king due attendance night and day.[1] He does not write as though Wyatt were as yet under arrest, — at least he was not then aware of it, — nor as if suspicion in any way inculpated his son in the charge upon which the others were arraigned. On the 11th of May Sir Henry Wyatt writes to Cromwell, having heard the day before by a letter from the minister the news of his son's arrest. In this letter of Wyatt's father's there is nothing to suggest the existence of a serious charge ; Sir Henry speaks of his son's deliverance as a thing of the near future, and asks Cromwell to admonish him to fly vice and to serve God better.[2] Under date of June 14 there is a second letter from Sir Henry to the minister, in which reference is made to Wyatt's release, which appears to have just occurred. Here also his father writes as if Wyatt's offence were of the nature of a quarrel, rather than aught against the king's security.[3]

In addition to these private notes there is a document of greater historical interest, in which some reference to the poet's present experience occurs. This is a paper drawn up for Cromwell's benefit, in which Sir William Kyngston, Keeper of the Tower, describes the speech and behavior of Anne Boleyn while a prisoner under his charge. This MS. is badly mutilated, and it is unfortunately impossible to say with any certainty in

[1] Calendar of State Papers, x. 819. Sir Hen. Wiat to his son Thos. Wiat. Considers himself most unfortunate that he can not go nor ride without danger to his life, or do his duty to the King in this dangerous time that his Grace has suffered by false traitors. Desires his son to give the King due attendance night and day. "I pray to God give him grace long to be with him and about him that hath found out this matter [Cromwell?], which hath been given him of God, and the false traitors to be punished according to justice to the example of others." Allington, May 7, 1536.

[2] Ibid., 840 (printed in Ald. ed., p. xx).

[3] Ibid., x. 1131 (printed in Ald. ed., p. xxi).

what connection the references to Wyatt occur.[1] Kyngston evidently informs the queen of the cause of Wyatt's imprisonment; and the mutilation makes a provoking break in the narrative. One is indeed tempted to complete the defective lines, — perhaps to the effect that Wyatt struck "one [with] his fist the other day and is here now but ma[ny think he will soon be pardoned]." Anne jokes further on because the male prisoners have no one to make their beds, suggesting that they might make ballads at least; and both Anne and Mistress Kyngston agree that Master Wyatt is the one to do this. There is, so far as we can see, no hint that the charges upon which Anne and the poet were respectively arraigned were in any way connected.

If we possessed no other data than the letters and the paper just referred to, we might dismiss the question of Wyatt's offence as settled; but the suspicions aroused by his imprisonment at just this time, and his earlier intimate relations with Anne Boleyn, are strengthened by the discovery of certain letters written by a courtier of the time. Again we have recourse to the correspondence of Lord Lisle, still deputy of Calais. The writer of the letters is one John Hussey, a gentleman of Henry's court; he probably reflects the impression of his associates. The first of these letters, under date of London, May 12, 1536, contains the following : —

[1] Calendar of State Papers, x. 798. Sir Wm. Kyngston to Cromwell. (A letter badly mutilated, concerning the speech and behaviour of Anne, then a prisoner in the Tower.) [Extracts therefrom.]
" . . . sent for me and sayd, I here say my Lord my . . . here; it ys trowth, sayd I. I am very glad, sayd s[he] . . . bothe be so ny to gether, and I showed hyr here was . . . Weston and Brerton, and she made very gud countenans . . . I also sayd Mr. Page and Wyet wase mo than she sayd he ha . . . one hys fyst tother day and ys here now bot ma . . . I shalle desyre you to bayre a letter from me . . . [to master] Secretary . . . [sh]e hathe asked my wyfe whether hony body makes theyr beddes, [and m]y wyf ansured ,and sayd, Nay, I warant you; then she say[d] [the]y myght make balettes well now, bot there ys non bot . . . de that can do it. Yese sayd my wyf, Master Wyett by . . . sayd trew." [Written in May, 1536.]

3

" . . . Today Mr. Norreys, Weston, Bryerton, and Markes have been arraigned, and are judged to be drawn, hanged, and quartered. They shall die tomorrow or Monday. Anne the queen, and her brother, shall be arraigned in the Tower, some think tomorrow, but on Monday at the furthest, and that they will suffer there immediately 'for divers considerations, which are not yet known.' Mr. Payge and Mr. W[y]at are in the Tower, but it is thought without danger of life, though Mr. Payge is banished the King's court for ever."[1]

Upon the 13th May, Hussey again writes : —

"Here are so many tales I cannot tell what to write. This day, some say, young Weston shall escape, and some that none shall die but the Queen and her brother; others, that Wyat and Mr. Payge are as like to suffer as the others. The saying now is that those who shall suffer shall die when the Queen and her brother go to execution; but I think they shall all suffer. If any escape it will be young Weston, for whom importunate suit is made."[2]

Writing again to Lord Lisle, on the 19th May, Hussey says :

"Lord Rocheford, Mr. Norreys, Bruriton, Weston, and Markes suffered with the axe on the scaffold at Tower Hill on Wednesday the 17th, and died very charitably. The Queen suffered with sword this day within the Tower, upon a new scaffold, and died boldly. . . . Mr. Payge and Mr. Wyat remain in the Tower."[3]

Upon the same day he writes to Lady Lisle : —

"Mr. Paige and young Wyat are in the Tower. What shall become of them God best knoweth."[4]

From this correspondence it will be seen that Wyatt's connection with the other offenders was generally taken for granted by the circle which Hussey represents. This supposition is still more clearly expressed in a note from Chapuis, the Austrian ambassador, to the English ambassador, resident at Vienna, wherein he says : —

---

[1] Calendar of State Papers, x. 855.   [3] Ibid., 919.
[2] Ibid., 865.   [4] Ibid., 920.

"There are still two gentlemen [Wyatt and Page] detained on her [Anne's] account."[1]

This letter also bears date of 19th May.

That both these gentlemen were in error in regard to the nature of the charge upon which Wyatt was imprisoned, is not beyond the limits of possibility. It was a time of excitement and suspicion. There must have been a thousand rumors in the air. Hussey says : "Here are so many tales I cannot tell what to write ; " and the fact of Wyatt's sudden arrest, occurring simultaneously with that of the alleged conspirators, would naturally give rise to such conjectures, whether true or false. Whatever the charge or the offence, the matter was soon settled, and by the 14th June, as we have already seen, Wyatt had his liberty.

Here our original investigations must for the present end, as the publication of the "Calendars," naturally a work of time, reaches (July, 1888) only as far as vol. x.

From Wyatt's statement in the oration already cited, we learn that he was appointed to a command in the army under the Duke of Norfolk, and ordered into Lancashire to oppose the rising under Lord Darcy. This appointment he received soon after his acquittal of the charges on which he had been imprisoned, and seems designedly to attest the continuance of Henry's favor and his unbroken confidence and esteem. In the following year Wyatt was appointed high sheriff of Kent " for a special confidence in such a busy time."[2]

There is considerable uncertainty as to when Wyatt received the honor of knighthood. Nott says in 1536, and quotes the *Cotton MS.* and an entry in Heralds' College, in the following note : —

" Sir Thomas Wyatt was dubbed Knight on Easter-day, 18th of March, 1536. *Cotton MS. Claudius, C. iii.* In the Heralds' Col-

---

[1] Calendar of State Papers, x. 909 (taken from the Vienna Archives).
[2] Wyatt's Defence : Nott, p. 300 ; Ald. ed., p. lxxxvii.

lege is this notice : Partition of the Knights' money. Sir Thomas Wyatt and Sir William Weste xxxv s. to the King at Arms v s. and to the Heralds 11s. 6d. Anno H. VIII. xxvii. at Westminster. Item, To Mr. Garter, for registring of the said Knights, Sir Thomas Wyatt and Sir William Weste, iiii s." [1]

But the editor of the Aldine edition quotes the entry in the *Cotton MS.* thus : —

" Sir Thomas Wyatt, dubbed on Easterday anno 28, the 18 [28] day of March, 1536." [2]

Now " anno 28 " would indicate the year 1537, not 1536, as Henry began to reign April 22, 1509, and March of 1536 would fall in *anno* 27 of Henry's reign.

Moreover Easter fell on the 16th April in 1536, and not in March, as the record seems to assert. It is strange, too, if 1536 be the correct date of this event, that Wyatt receives no title other than " master " or " esquire " in any of the papers of that year. The earliest writing found as yet in which the title of "knight" is employed happens to be a letter of Cromwell's dated 6th of June, — not the 29th of June, as the editor of the Aldine edition states, — 1537. [3] It is more than probable that Wyatt received the honor shortly before starting on his mission to Spain, in the early part of 1537. He is still designated as " esquire," even in the paper of instructions given by the king immediately before his departure. [4]

Sir Thomas Wyatt served his king as resident ambassador at the Court of Charles V. in Spain from June in 1537 until June or July of 1539. During this period of two years it is possible that he made one or more journeys to England in order to lay certain matters of superior importance more clearly before his master. The object of his mission was to pacify the emperor, who was more or less exasperated by the treatment to which his aunt, Queen Catharine, had been subjected, and also to lessen,

---

1 Nott, p. xxviii, foot-note.   8 Nott, p 324.
2 Ald. ed., p. xxiii.   4 Ibid., p. 312.

if he might, the likelihood of Charles's espousing the cause of Mary, and advancing her claim to the throne of England.

The leading events in Wyatt's life while on this embassy are so well known as to call for little remark here. For Wyatt personally, the coming of the two special envoys, Haynes and Bonner, in May of 1538, was destined to affect in an unexpected and troublesome manner the circumstances of his later life. Not only did their conduct there embarrass him in the accomplishment of his mission, but, instigated by spite or envy, certain charges were perpetrated by Bonner against the poet, criticising severely Wyatt's conduct, and reflecting upon his honor and his loyalty. The negotiations with the emperor, while unsuccessful in the main, were nevertheless so conducted by Wyatt as to win Henry's approbation and substantial expression of his approval. From the correspondence still preserved we gather that Cromwell was at this time the best friend that Wyatt had. He looked with considerable care after the property of the absent ambassador, who seems to have left his private affairs in some confusion, and at the same time he assisted Wyatt very materially by his recommendations to the king. In February of 1539 Cromwell writes to him that he has procured for the poet grant of the Friary of Alresford,[1] — this occurring on the dissolution of the monasteries. One of Cromwell's letters, written in January of the same year, 1539, permits a new glimpse of Wyatt's character too important to be overlooked. Promising to remit money as he may need, the minister accompanies his promise with a mild rebuke, advising him " nevertheless, that I think your gentle frank heart doth much impoverish you. When you have money you are content to depart with it and lend it, as you did lately two hundred ducats to Mr. Hobby, the which I think had no need of them ; for he had large furnishment of money at his departure hence, and likewise at his return." [2]

A certain remark of Wyatt's own, with a bearing on his experience in Spain, is also of sufficient importance to demand a

---

[1] Nott, p. 345.   [2] Ibid., p. 344 ; Ald. ed., p. xxix.

place. At a later time, defending himself against the imputation cast by Bonner upon the sincerity of his religious professions, Wyatt says : —

"What men judge of me abroad, this may be a great token, that the King's Majesty and his Council know what hazard I was in in Spain with the Inquisition, only by speaking against the Bishop of Rome, where peradventure Bonner would not have bid such a brunt. The Emperor had much ado to save me, and yet that made me not to hold my peace, when I might defend the King's deed against him, and improve his naughtiness."[1]

It must be noted, too, that during the latter part of his stay abroad Wyatt was full of longing to return to England. He realized the futility of his efforts with the emperor, was perplexed by complications in his private affairs, and was fully conscious of the ill-will of Bonner, and of the existence of the latter's charges, which might prove of great annoyance and peril to him. In addition to these embarrassments, Wyatt was called upon to mourn the loss of his father ; and the impression made upon the poet by his death we have already seen reflected in the letter to his son.

Upon Wyatt's return to England in July of 1539 he at once demanded an investigation of the charges preferred against him. Cromwell, however, assured him that such an investigation had been already made, and the whole matter dismissed as trivial and without foundation. Sir Thomas was now permitted to return to his home at Allington, where he busied himself with family concerns and the improvement of his estate. But he was not permitted long to enjoy the seclusion of domestic life. Towards the end of 1539 Charles V. made a journey to the Netherlands, passing through France upon his way. To Henry it was a matter of prime importance to be informed of all that might occur upon this progress, for he was suspicious of the emperor's designs, and more or less in fear of his future movements. It became necessary, therefore, to appoint some person

[1] Wyatt's Defence : Nott, p. 294 ; Ald. ed., p. lxxx.

of unusual foresight and experience, who, in the character of special envoy, should carefully watch the progress of events and report to Henry every fact of interest that might happen. For a mission of this character no one among Henry's courtiers was better qualified than Sir Thomas Wyatt. Admirably equipped with the insight into Charles's character gained by him when resident at the Spanish Court, and with the additional advantage of possessing the esteem and friendship of the emperor, Wyatt was appointed to this new post of honor and of difficulty, and entered immediately upon the fulfilment of its duties.

He arrived at Paris in November. Thence he proceeded to Blois, where he obtained an interview with Francis, and then hastened to join the emperor, December 10th, at Chaterault. In January the Imperial Court was at Paris ; thence it removed to Brussels. In March and April Wyatt was with the emperor at Ghent. In May, after having repeatedly solicited his own recall, he was allowed to return to England. Again Sir Thomas was received with tokens of royal approbation, and we have no cause for doubting that the king was satisfied with the way in which the mission had been performed. Wyatt's correspondence while absent on this embassy has been preserved,[1] and his official letters to Cromwell and to Henry afford unusually interesting reading. He describes minutely his interviews with king and emperor, remarks with sagacity upon the political situation, and tells his story withal in a way which adds the charm of personality to the value which the papers would otherwise possess historically. A study of this correspondence leaves no doubt as to Wyatt's eminent qualifications for this mission, and establishes his unusual ability in diplomatic service.

It was in May of the year 1540 that Wyatt arrived once more in England. In about a month came the downfall of the powerful minister, Wyatt's good friend, Cromwell. It was not unexpected. It is a singular fact that Cromwell had himself warned his friends of the ruin which he, as clearly as any one,

---

[1] Printed by Nott in his appendix.

saw approaching ; and it is not at all unlikely that this foreboding
of a coming danger was one reason for Wyatt's persistency in
pressing for his recall from France. -There was indeed ground
for disquietude, for the party which had overthrown the minister
would naturally direct their hostility further, and perhaps attack
the fallen statesman's friends, among whom Wyatt was conspicuous. We have already had occasion to note the friendly
services which Cromwell had often tendered him. His letters
to the absent ambassador are always full of kindly feeling, which
finds expression in spite of the official nature of the papers.
It is to "my very loving friend" that these documents are
addressed, and in like fashion subscribed. In fact Cromwell
had ever been "good lord" to Wyatt, as the expression ran,
and it was not improbable that the ruin of his powerful patron
might involve his own.

Whether Wyatt anticipated it or not, he was now exposed to
real and serious danger. His old enemy Bonner had been
made bishop of London, and was therefore in a position to
renew the old animosity and to prosecute his revengeful plans.
This he did ; and the former allegations against Wyatt's loyalty
were once more trumped forth. In spite of the complete
acquittal in which the previous investigation had resulted,
Henry, ever suspicious of the faithfulness of any subject, lent
his ear to the bishop's representations and had the knight
arrested and imprisoned in the Tower. Such undeserved treatment and apparent ingratitude on his sovereign's part were not
without effect on Wyatt's spirit. As he wrote in the verses
addressed to Sir Francis Bryan,[1] and as he declared in his
speech before the judges,[2] though the wound might in time be
healed, a cruel scar would always remain to show the depth of
his hurt.

Wyatt was thrown into the Tower about the beginning of
1541, but it was several months before he was brought to trial.

---

[1] Nott, p. 72; Ald. ed., p. 174.
[2] Nott, p. 292; Ald. ed., p. lxxvii.

The charges lodged by Bonner two or three years before had been originally presented in a letter to Cromwell written while Bonner was at Blois, and bearing date of 2d September, 1538.[1] Herein were set forth ten articles, comprising various trivial attacks upon the ambassador's character both in private life and in the discharge of public duty; certain remarks were quoted, construed to imply disloyalty to the king; moreover complaints were made of the mistreatment which Bonner fancied he himself had experienced at Wyatt's hands. In addition to this collection of insinuations, Wyatt was alleged to have carried on a treasonable correspondence with Reginald Pole, an Englishman of the highest family, a grandson of the Duke of Clarence, who, because of his hostility to the project of Henry's divorce, had been obliged to flee from England and take refuge in Rome, where he had been made cardinal by the pope.

In accordance with the custom of that day, the accused was requested by the Privy Council to draw up in writing a defence, setting forth and explaining, for the establishment of his own innocence, all the incidents occurring while on his embassy in Spain which might be construed as evidence of treason. He remained in ignorance of the specific charges lodged against him; he must answer blindfolded, in a sense, yet so clearly and so conclusively, and with such exactness, as to remove all doubt of innocence. This dubious command Wyatt obeyed at once, skilfully, and apparently with success.[2] The formal trial followed, and Wyatt was brought before his judges. He was allowed neither counsel nor witnesses, nor permitted to cross-examine his accusers. In a single speech he was obliged to refute all allegations and to remove from the minds of the council the misconception and prejudice which Bonner might have succeeded in arousing. Wyatt was in a difficult case; but he was equal to the occasion. Never did a man under accusation of high crimes plead his cause with greater vigor or more successfully. Not content with a complete refutation of Bonner's

---

[1] Ald. ed., p. xxxv.   [2] Nott, p. 277; Ald. ed., p. lxi.

scandalous charges, he proceeded further to unmask his ac-
cuser's character, and attacked him in turn with such keenness
and such humor that he not only procured a triumphant acquittal by his masterly defence, but heaped confusion on his
adversary, and at the same time won new fame as a man of
letters.[1]

The trial took place probably in June; in the course of the
following month the king bestowed upon the poet a grant of
lands in Lambeth, and in the early part of 1542 made him high
steward of the manor of Maidstone, also granting him estates
in Dorsetshire and Somersetshire in exchange for others of less
value in Kent.[2]

Wyatt was now once more living in retirement at his pleasant
home of Allington; and here he evidently hoped to spend the
remainder of his days in the enjoyment of those quiet delights
which he pictures in the Satires. He had had enough of the
life at Court, and could rightly estimate the doubtful happiness
and vain security of those who —

> "Stand . . . upon the slipper top
> Of high estate."

Of his occupation during this period of his life he writes
thus to his friend John Poins: —

> "This maketh me at home to hunt and hawk;
> And in foul weather at my book to sit;
> In frost and snow, then with my bow to stalk:
> No man doth mark whereso I ride or go:
> In lusty leas at liberty I walk;
> And of these news I feel nor weal, nor woe." [3]

Part of the poet's leisure was devoted to the education of his
sister's son, Henry Lee. This was also the period of the paraphrase of the Penitential Psalms, which seems to Dr. Nott's mind

---

[1] Nott, p. 284; Ald. ed., p. lxix.
[2] Hutchins's Dorsetshire, i. 189; Ald. ed., p. xliv.
[3] Nott's ed., p. 90; Ald. ed., p. 193.

"written not as an exercise of his skill as a poet, but to express a Christian's sorrow for the levities and errors of his youth," [1] — a surmise far-fetched, to say the least. That Wyatt's mind should be sobered and deeply impressed by the circumstances of the years in which he lived, was to be expected; and that, with these impressions quickened by the recent peril from which he had but just emerged, he should derive comfort and satisfaction from a work like this, need not seem surprising. But it was no act of penitence, or of penance, any more than in the case of Surrey, who paraphrased Ecclesiastes and several of the Psalms of David; or of those French poets — almost, if not quite, contemporaries — who turned their talents in the same direction.

In the autumn of 1542 ambassadors from Charles V. arrived in England, and Wyatt was at once commissioned by the king to meet the envoys at Falmouth for the purpose of conducting them to London. The performance of this honorable service cost the poet his life. The weather was bad, and Wyatt, in his zeal, had overheated himself by rapid riding. He fell sick of a fever while resting at Sherborne; the fever took a malignant turn, and after a few days' illness Wyatt died. A friend of the poet's, by the name of Horsey, who lived in the neighborhood of Sherborne, had hastened to his bedside at the first news of Wyatt's sickness, and it was by the hands of this friend that the last offices for the dead knight were performed. On the 11th October, 1542, Wyatt's remains were laid in the vault of the Horsey family, in the great church at Sherborne; but no inscription remains to tell us precisely where the poet lies.

Numerous epitaphs from the pens of contemporary writers give proof of the general esteem and appreciation with which Wyatt's character and services were regarded. Most notable of these, perhaps, were a short poetic tribute from the poet Surrey, and a Latin elegy from the hand of Sir John Mason, — the latter a friend of the poet, and himself a noted scholar and

[1] Nott, p. lxviii.

writer. Without attempting even a brief summary of these expressions of commendation and regret, it may suffice to say
that all unite especially in praise of Wyatt's frank and generous
spirit, and of the strong integrity of his manly character.

In his person Wyatt was tall and handsome, with a com-
manding presence. From his boyhood he was noted for cour-
age and coolness, — two qualities which not only characterized
his after career abroad, but stood him in good stead when a
defendant at the bar of the Privy Council. He was a successful courtier at a time when to retain the royal favor was a more
delicate business than the capture of it; but Wyatt's continuance in the king's good grace was due rather to the transparent
honesty and marked ability of the man than to a succession
of lucky hits or to a course of systematic cunning. Wyatt was
sagacious and far-seeing in matters of public policy. He had
a keen wit, and many are the anecdotes remaining of what
"Wyatt told to the king." Of special interest is it to note that
Sir Thomas was a man of letters; and if little has thus far been
said touching this side of his career, it is because it seemed better
to treat of that apart, in a portion of our essay entirely devoted
to a consideration of the poet's work. Wyatt was remarkable for
linguistic attainment among the scholars of that day; not only
familiar with the languages and literatures of France, Italy, and
Spain, he was thoroughly at home among the classic writers, and
was spoken of as *splendide doctus* by an eminent scholar of his
time. That in Wyatt's character worthy of most emphatic recognition, however, is the high ideal of life presented in all his
later works, and, so far as we may judge, exemplified in his own
career. No indecency mars his poetry; no word of his suggests the tolerance or the condoning of a vicious thing. He
honored virtue; he loved sincerity. "If you will seem honest,
be honest; or else seem as you are," is the counsel he gave his
son; and what he urged upon the boy, that quality his contemporaries unite in attributing to him.

Wyatt's wife, Elizabeth, survived him, and afterwards married

Sir Edward Warner. Sir Thomas left a son, known as Sir Thomas Wyatt the younger. At fifteen years of age he married the daughter of Sir William Hawte; and it was at this period that the two remarkable letters already quoted were addressed him by his father. He became a friend and intimate of the poet Surrey, and followed with distinction under his command in the war with France. He evidently inherited the same bold spirit and carelessness of danger which had marked his father's earlier years. After the death of Edward VI. he remained an uncompromising Protestant, and during Mary's reign engaged in the rash attempt to raise the Lady Jane Grey to the throne. The rebellion failing, Wyatt was made prisoner, and on the 11th April, 1554, paid the penalty of treason at the block. With this event the Wyatt family lost, for the most part, their wealth and their position; although in the reign of Elizabeth they were restored to favor, and a portion of their old possessions at last came back to them.

Part Second.

WYATT'S POEMS.

Part Second.

WYATT'S POEMS.

———◆———

A. The Text.

IN passing from the record of Wyatt's life to a consideration
of his poetry it is desirable and even necessary to glance
for a moment at the history and condition of the text.

With the latter part of Queen Mary's reign there came an
innovation into English literary circles. The poetical miscellany arrived. These volumes of selected poems at once
achieved a great popularity, and edition after edition fell from
the press. First in point of date and of importance is the
collection known as Tottel's Miscellany; the first edition appeared in June of 1557, was followed by another in the following month, and that by a third and a fourth, and so on
until the book had reached its eighth edition in 1587. This
volume has reappeared in the series of English Reprints edited
by Edward Arbèr. Arber's reprint of Tottel's Miscellany
(Birmingham, 1870) reproduces the original edition of 5th
June, 1557, collated with the second of 31st July, same year.
The Miscellany contains forty poems by Henry Howard, Earl
of Surrey, ninety-six by Sir Thomas Wyatt, forty from the hand
of Nicholas Grimald, and one hundred and thirty-four by uncertain authors. Wyatt's translation of the Penitential Psalms
had been published in December of 1549; but Tottel's Mis-

4

cellany, appearing fifteen years subsequent to the poet's death, formed, the first edition of Wyatt's miscellaneous poems that we possess; and it is for this reason that Tottel's publication is of special interest here.

Of the various editions of Wyatt's works appearing since that day, by far the most important is that edited by the Rev. G. F. Nott, D. D., forming the second volume of The Works of Henry Howard, Earl of Surrey, and Sir Thomas Wyatt the Elder, London, 1815–16. Dr. Nott's bulky quarto volume contains an enormous mass of material zealously collected by the editor, who seems to have exhausted all sources of information in his day accessible. One finds here extensive extracts from historical papers of special interest; long quotations from other writers contemporary with the poet; copies of letters and State documents important and necessary in the study of Wyatt's life and works. The labor expended and the conscientious care exhibited are really remarkable, and call for more generous recognition than has frequently been accorded. Nott's work must always remain a standard book of reference for those who busy themselves with the study of this poet. The text which Dr. Nott has followed in his edition of Wyatt's poems differs materially from that found in the Miscellany. It is a text based upon the reading of certain MSS. which Nott first brought to public notice, and which are especially valuable in that they bring for the first time to our acquaintance a considerable number of Wyatt's poems never before published.

First in importance is the so-called Harington MS., found in the possession of a certain Dr. Harington, of Bath. " It is a small folio, consisting originally of about 270 pages, some of which have been torn away, and some mutilated. It was Sir Thomas Wyatt's own MS., and, with the exception of a few pieces, . . . contains his poems exclusively. The first part of the volume, as far as page 121, was written evidently by an amanuensis; but Wyatt himself seems to have corrected carefully the whole of what had been transcribed, inserting such

lines and words as had been omitted, and frequently making
alterations. He has added also his name in the margin of
almost every page; sometimes at full length, sometimes giving
his Christian name, Tho : or his initials, T. V. only. The
pieces which follow after page 121, as far as page 207, are in
Sir Thomas Wyatt's own handwriting throughout, the two
letters from Spain excepted, which are copied into the book
in the handwriting of Sir Thomas Wyatt the son." [1]

"All the poems are marked with numbers at the top, with
the word 'Enter' subjoined; as thus, '1. Enter.' '2. Enter,'
etc. The numbers go as far as six, which includes the two
letters from Spain. No. 5 comprehends the Satires; and No.
4 the Paraphrase of the Seven Penitential Psalms, with that
of the 37th Psalm. The smaller pieces seem to have been
classed under No. 1; No. 2 contains the Sonnets; and No. 3
the larger Odes. Such appears to have been the general principle of the arrangement, which being thus systematical, was
made probably with a view to publication." [2]

This valuable MS. came into the possession of the Harington
family as early as the time of Queen Elizabeth, as is proved
by the handwriting of Sir John Harington, which occurs frequently in it. The MS. has had a varying history. [2]

A second MS. text, found in the library of the Duke of
Devonshire, was used by Dr. Nott in preparing his edition.
This MS. is a small folio of 225 pages, containing Wyatt's poems
almost exclusively, and is written for the most part in one
handwriting with considerable care and neatness. [8] Nott conjectures that this second Wyatt MS. was the property of Wyatt's
sister, Margaret Lee, or of the Duchess of Richmond, the sister
of Surrey; for the names of both these ladies occur in the
book. This MS. is of special value as containing several poems
found nowhere else. [4] A third MS. is obscurely referred to by
Dr. Nott under the title of Harington MS. No. 2; but he
specifies nothing as to its character or value.

---

[1] Nott, Preface, i. [2] Ibid., iv. [8] Ibid., vii. [4] Ibid., ix.

Since the publication of Nott's quarto, in 1816, several editions of less note have appeared, sometimes published in connection with the works of Surrey, sometimes forming a single volume of themselves. In nearly every case the editor has followed Tottel's reading, and ignored, so far as possible, the text given by Dr. Nott. Among these editions are found the following : —

Poetical Works of Sir Thomas Wyatt, edited by Robert Bell. London, 1854.

The Aldine Edition of Wyatt's Works, edited by James Yeowell. London (no date).

The Riverside Edition, published by Houghton, Mifflin, & Co., Cambridge (U. S. A.), 1880.

The editions mentioned are all of the same type, and while not the only ones that have appeared, have been selected as more generally accessible. Bell occasionally adopts a reading found in Nott, while usually preferring Tottel's text. He says :

"The general superiority of Tottel's edition consists in the presentation of a more perfect metre ; and it is on that account principally followed throughout." [1]

The Aldine follows Tottel without variation. The Riverside is practically a reprint of the Aldine.

It may be asked with reason why preference has so generally been accorded by the editors to Tottel's reading when that of the Harington MS. would seem to possess the superior authority of Wyatt's ownership and correction. The answer given in the remark of Bell's, which has been quoted, is insufficient. Smoothness of rhythm is no absolute criterion in critically selecting an authoritative text. The two texts must be more carefully examined and compared.

Tottel gives no information regarding the origin of his text ; but from the character of its variations from the Harington, it

---

[1] Bell's ed., p. 80 (foot-note).

may unhesitatingly be pronounced younger than the MS. This point will be again referred to further on. The differences in the reading of the Miscellany and the manuscript may be classified as follows : —

I. Changes made for metrical purposes. Such are re-arrangement in the order ; the addition or the omission of a syllable or syllables ; the exchange of a word or words for others which fit the measure better.

II. Variations in the phraseology necessitated by a change in the thought interpreted.

III. The substitution of one unimportant word for another, — often to be explained as an error of the copyist or printer.

In cases I. and II. the variations may prove to be the later critical work of the poet himself, or they may be the result of editorial revision at the time that Tottel's Miscellany was prepared ; a third possibility remains, — that the original text became corrupt while in MS. circulation before the publisher obtained possession of it. Dr. Nott believes that Tottel's editor wilfully falsified the text.[1] Later editors and commentators find it incredible that the poet should not himself have employed the means to secure a smoother verse, if the faults were so apparent and the remedy so easily at hand that an ordinary book-publisher, fifteen years after the poet's death, should deem it necessary to correct his lines, and then succeed in accomplishing the task so well.[2]

But the matter is not so easily to be disposed of. In the first place, it should not be forgotten that Wyatt fills a peculiar posi-

[1] Nott, p. 537 (notes to Sonnets I., II., III.).

[2] Kann man sich mit Nott der Ansicht zuneigen, dass ein Dichter wie Wyatt seine Verse in einer oftmals dem rhythmischen Gefühle Hohn sprechenden Form für würdig erachtet habe, ihren Lauf unter der vornehmsten Gesellschaft anzutreten, während schon fünfzehn Jahre nachher ein gewöhnlicher Buchhändler dieselben Verse so dürftig fand, dass er sie nicht in unveränderter Gestalt, sondern nur überarbeitet und überpolirt in seinen Band vermischter Gedichte aufnahm ? ! — RUDOLF ALSCHER : *Sir Thomas Wyatt, etc. (Wiener Beiträge zur deut. u. eng. Philologie, Heft i.), p. 49.*

tion in the history of the development of English poetry, which none of the other prominent writers of his day can share. He was practically the first of the modern English poets; and although versed in the methods of Petrarch's art, and familiar with the laws of the French and Italian schools, Wyatt was by no means so exact a versemaker as other poets of his age. In his earlier work his versification is crude enough, and his verses resemble those of his predecessor, Stephen Hawes, much more closely than they do the smoother lines of Surrey. Even in his later poems, notably in the Paraphrase of the Seven Penitential Psalms, there is at times a rawness in his treatment of metre that is positively harsh and inharmonious. Wyatt should not be judged in the category with the later members of a school which he himself had in a sense founded. Any one of them, perhaps, — and there was a numerous company, — possessed a more delicate sense of the laws of rhythm than did he; and they were better qualified to avoid his errors, and to improve upon his methods, because he had preceded them and prepared the way before them.

Again, between the writing of Wyatt's love-poems and the publication of Tottel's Miscellany a longer period than fifteen years had intervened. At least twenty-five years, if not more, had elapsed since Wyatt wrote the earlier of his songs and sonnets, in which the greater part of the variations are to be found. Moreover, following Wyatt's lead, a whole company of "courtly makers" had arisen, with the Earl of Surrey at their head, and the average of public taste and criticism was measurably higher. The pronunciation of many words, not absolutely fixed when Wyatt began to write, had become settled in a generally accepted form, — possibly during the poet's lifetime, certainly by the end of the quarter century. For example, we find in the Harington MS., occurring in one of the poems preserved to us in Wyatt's own handwriting, the verse, —

"You! that in love find luck and *abundance*."[1]

[1] Nott, p. 5.

It is evident here that the poet accented the closing word in the old, familiar style of Chaucer, *ábundánce*, with a noticeable secondary accent on the final syllable ; and so we have the rhyme, *ábundánce, mischánce, óbservánce, advánce*. But in Tottel's Miscellany we find the verse running, —

> " Ye that in love find luck and *sweet abúndance*." [1]

No change was then thought necessary, however, in the accent of *óbservánce*.

Secondly, respecting the editorship of Tottel's Miscellany. We are by no means certain that this collection of miscellaneous poetry was prepared for the printer by an ordinary book-publisher. More than one fact points forcibly to the surmise that in the editor of that volume we have to recognize a well-known poet of Mary's reign ; namely, Nicholas Grimald, who was born about the year 1519, and who died previous to 1562. He was a contributor to the pages of the Miscellany, forty of his poems appearing in the first edition. The grounds for this surmise in reference to his editing the book are, briefly, these : [2] —

I. Grimald had been in business relations with Tottel previously. In 1556 Tottel printed Grimald's translation of Cicero's *De Officiis*.

II. It is probably due to the fact that Grimald was chaplain to the Bishop of Ely that Tottel was able to put *cum privilegio* on that book.

III. The only poems suppressed in the second edition of the Miscellany are Grimald's own.

IV. The name Nicholas Grimald disappears after the first revision, and is represented by " N. G."

V. Thirty poems by Grimald of a *personal* nature are removed, to make place for thirty-nine by uncertain authors.

Nicholas Grimald was not a great poet, but he was a clever versifier. He was, judging from his poems in the Miscellany, a

---

[1] Tottel, p. 36; Ald. ed., p. 5.
[2] Tottel's Miscellany : Arber's Introduction, p. xv.

rigid follower of the ancient classic style in versification as in allusion. He adheres with unvarying strictness to the iambic verse, and allows few freedoms. If Grimald *were* the editor of Tottel's, it is not improbable that he might consider as a part of his editorial duty the moulding of the dead poet's verses into what he regarded, and what, by that time, his contemporary critics would regard, their proper form, in obedience to the rules which he and they so carefully observed. What has here been said, however, is not so much for the purpose of establishing a theory respecting the editorship of Tottel's Miscellany as to prepare the way for a fairer discussion of the merits of the respective texts than has hitherto been accorded; and this much by way of establishing a possibility that has been overlooked by some of the editors and critics who have spoken authoritatively upon the case.

A word is necessary now regarding the condition of the Harington text. Dr. Nott has described the MS. as follows : —

"The pieces which follow after page 121, as far as page 207 [viz., those in Wyatt's own handwriting], . . . are written carelessly, and have frequent erasures and alterations, which prove that Wyatt made use of the book latterly for the rough draughts only of his cómpositions. This will account for the imperfect state in which many of them appear."[1]

Thus, according to Nott's own admission, there is doubt as to the reliability of the text in cases which he thus specifies, — doubt not of the genuineness of the MS. reading, but as to the propriety of following that reading; for if the "carelessly written" poems between pages 121 and 207 are merely "rough draughts", afterwards completed and put in circulation in a form quite different, we should do best implicitly to follow Tottel's reading, and discard the text which Dr. Nott has offered us. The matter can be settled only by a critical examination of the variations; and no decision can be given until

---

[1] Nott, Preface, ii.

the two MSS. employed by Nott, and especially the Harington, shall have been seen and studied. The writer regrets to say that he has been unable to gain access to the original texts, and therefore confines himself to a brief examination of one or more poems, which may furnish an illustration of some of the points asserted.

For this purpose we turn to the *Song of Iopas* (Nott, p. 60 ; Tottel (Arber's reprint), p. 93 ; Ald. ed., p. 159). We examine first the variations which correct a metrical irregularity in the MS. text. Such is that found in verse 3, where Nott gives the MS. reading : —

" That mighty Atlas *did teach*, the supper lasting long."

Tottel rids the verse of the superfluous syllable thus : —

" That mighty Atlas *taught* the supper lasting long."

The use of the form with *did* is common with Wyatt. In the *Complaint of the Absence of his Love* (N. 56 ; T. 73 ; A. 154), we find several instances all retained by Tottel ; these are as follows : *did lose* (v. 35) ; *did leave* (v. 44) ; *did lead* (v. 68) ; *did bring* (v. 76) ; *did make* (v. 86). The same form occurs in the preceding verse of the Iopas poem, *did force* (v. 2). It seems apparent therefore that the alteration was made to avoid the roughness in the verse. But when originally written, an elision must have been intended of *mighty Atlas*, which brings the line within proper bounds. A similar change occurs in the verse which follows ; the MS. reading : —

" With crisped locks, on golden harp, Iopas sang in *his* song."

Tottel drops the possessive, although the elision *in his* is by no means difficult. In neither of these cases have we as yet any right to refer the alteration to Tottel's editor ; assuming that Nott here gives us the correct reading of Wyatt's autograph text, the possibility that Wyatt himself corrected that text at a later period is always before us.   Verse 11 stands thus in the MS. :

"And it is called by name the first moving heaven."

Tottel inserts a syllable and reads : —

"And it is called by name the first *and* moving heaven."

It seems improbable that this insertion was made by the poet. It is not what he means to say.   All the "heavens" of which he speaks are *moving* heavens ; he merely designates this as the first of the series.   In verse 37 we find the expression repeated, "in the first moving heaven ; " and so "the first moving sky," in verse 73 ; and again "the first moving heaven " in verse 76. In all these cases the connective is superfluous, and spoils the sense ; verse 11, although it lacks a syllable of the regular number, is not disagreeable to the ear, and hardly calls for such an emendation at the cost of clearness.   It may well be doubted that the poet is here responsible for the change.   The reading of verse 12, as given us by Nott, is lacking by a complete measure ; the verse is an alexandrine instead of a septinar, which is to be expected in accordance with the form adopted.   Where Nott reads : —

"The firmament is next, containing other seven,"

Tottel gives us the verse corrected thus : —

"The firmament is *pláced* next containing other seven."

It is possible that the missing word has been accidentally omitted in transcribing ; at any rate we must look to Tottel for the proper reading.   Verse 58 has also been changed to avoid a roughness in the metre of the original.   The MS. reading is this : —

"And so doth the next to the same that second is in order."

In the text of the Miscellany, the verse reads : —

"So doth the next *unto* the same that second is in order."

The verse as it stands in Tottel has rather an artificial tone ; it is not so characteristic of Wyatt as the former reading. The change is more suggestive of an editorial emendation than it is of a correction by the poet's own hand. The same may be said in regard to the alteration in verse 76, which the MS. gives : —

" Bé not 'bóut that axletree of the first moving heaven."

Tottel reads : —

" Be nót abóut   .   .   .   .   "

thus ridding the verse of the freedom known as initial truncation. It must be admitted that this freedom is not a frequent one with Wyatt ; still, it does occur : *e. g.*, in the Second Satire, —

" Práise Sir Tópas fór a nóble tále." — N. 89 ; T. 89 ; A. 192.

We come now to a second class of variations, which may be due to a simple error of the pen, or to a misunderstanding of the sense. Verse 20 in the MS. text stands thus : —

" Against the same dividing just the *round* by line direct."

In the Miscellany we find the word *ground* substituted for the word italicized. The poet is speaking of the vast sphere of the universe, and imagines a "line direct" extending from the North Pole star to its correspondent in the southern hemisphere. This direct line of course penetrates our own sphere, passes through its centre, and forms the earth's diameter. It therefore just divides the "round," which may be either the great sphere of the universe, or the globe itself. It will thus be seen that the word *round* has a significance here that is wanting in the word which Tottel uses to displace it. Somewhat similar is the case in verse 31, which is given in the MS. text, —

" And eke those erring seven in *circles* as they stray,"

where Tottel substitutes the singular in place of the plural form. As the poet here refers to the heavens of verse 26, and has in mind a series of parallel circles, seven in number, revolving on a common axis, it is manifestly more appropriate that he should in thinking of this complex revolution of the heavens, each in a plane of its own, employ the plural *circles* in speaking of them collectively. Bell here follows Nott; the other editions preserve Tottel's reading. The editor of the Miscellany has badly twisted the proper sense of verse 54. In the MS. the line stands, —

"And in the same the day his eye, the sun, therein he sticks."

The thought, robbed of its poetic figure, is clearly this. In this fourth circle the day has set his eye, — the sun. Tottel regards " the day his eye " as a possessive ; the subject of the sentence to be *circle ;* he then alters the pronoun to an ethical dative, *her,* which he makes refer to *circle.* We then have the remarkable line : —

"And in the same the dayes eye the sun, therein her sticks."

This is so manifest a blunder that all the editions mentioned adopt the MS. reading. Tottel has another manifest error in verse 61, where the MS. reads : —

" That sky is last, and *first* next us those ways hath gone."

Tottel alters the line to read : —

" That sky is last, and *fixt* next us   .   .   .   .   "

In addition to the variations here cited, a third group will be noticed, but less significant for our purpose, as not containing any clew to their origin, or any characteristic whereby to judge of their respective values. These variations are the following :

In verse 18, Nott reads " There be two points . . . . . . "
           Tottel,   " Two points there be . . . . . . "
"   "   23, Nott,   " And these *been* called the poles, *de-scribed . . .*"
           Tottel,   " And these *be* called the poles, *descried . . .*"

In verse 26, Nott has *doth ;*   Tottel *do.*
"   "   51,   "   " *bear'th ;*   "   *bears.*
"   "   55,   "   " *governeth ;*   "   *governs.*
"   "   67,   "   " *himselves ;*   "   *themselves.*
"   "   67,   "   " *been ;*   "   *be.*
"   "   76,   "   " *that ;*   "   *the.*

What shall our decision be then respecting the comparative merits of the texts? We have noted two classes of significant variations: I. Those made on metrical grounds. In one of these cases (v. 11) the sense of the passage seems to prove the alteration unjustifiable, and makes us doubt the possibility of its being the poet's work. In two other cases (v. 58, 76) the mechanical quality of the variation, and the fact that the MS. reading is not uncharacteristic of the poet's handiwork, leads us to the same conclusion. In two instances (v. 3, 4) an unnecessary alteration has been made to avoid a possible superfluity of syllables already provided against by an easy elision in both places. The only case (v. 12) in which we give Tottel's reading preference is of such a character as to suggest a very simple oversight on the part of the original writer (unless the omission be a transcriber's error), and does not throw discredit upon the general authority of the MS. II. The variations which are based on apparent misinterpretation, or else on carelessness in copying, speak strongly for the superiority of the MS. text.

It must now be borne in mind that the MS. text of this poem is in Wyatt's autograph; it is one of the number designated by Nott as "carelessly written," possibly a "rough draught," afterwards copied and corrected by the poet's own direction. It cannot be denied that some of the variations might have originated in this way; but the occurrence of others of a character forbidding such an assumption compels us to assert the authority of the Harington text, and to accept its reading.

Let us turn now to another poem in which material and significant variations may be found. We will take the sonnet, *How oft have I* (N. 13 ; T. 69 ; A. 14). The two versions run as follows : —

How oft have I, my dear and cruel foe,

Harington MS.	Tottel.
With those your eyes for to get peace and truce,	With my great pain to get some peace or truce,
Proffered you mine heart; but you do not use,	Given you my heart? but you do not use,
Among so high things, to cast your mind so low.	In so high things, to cast your mind so low.
If any other look for it, as ye trow,	If any other look for it, as you trow,

Their vain weak hope doth greatly them abuse :

| And thus I disdain that that ye refuse. | And that thus I disdain, that you refuse. |

It was once mine, it can no more be so.

| If I then it chase, nor it in you can find, | If you it chase, that it in you can find, |

In this exile, no manner of comfort,
Nor live alone, nor where he is called resort;
He may wander from his natural kind.
So shall it be great hurt unto us twain,
And yours the loss, and mine the deadly pain.

It happens that this particular poem is a translation of one of Petrarch's sonnets, — the 19th. *Mille fiate, o dolce mia guerrera,* and a comparison with the original is quite instructive. We give only those passages in which the principal variations occur : —

v. 2. " *Per aver co' begli occhi vostri pace.*" Petrarch.
"With those your eyes for to get peace and truce." Har. MS.
" With my great pain to get some peace or truce." Tottel.

v. 3. " *V' aggio proferto il cor; m' a voi non piace.*"
" Proffered you mine heart; but you do not use."
" Given . . . my . . . ."

v. 9. " *Or, s' io lo scaccio, ed e' non trova in voi.*"
" If I then it chase, nor it in you can find."
" . you (ʌ) . . . that . . . . . ."

We see at a glance that Tottel's version is the younger of the two. In v. 2, 9, where the thought has been completely changed, the text of the MS. is a literal translation of the original. The word *proffered* of v. 3 was evidently suggested to the translator by the presence of the Italian *proferto* in the line before him. In certain cases where two versions of a foreign original are preserved, we might be led to suppose the freer version of the two a first unsatisfactory attempt which had suggested a second trial, resulting in a closer imitation of the work translated. It is evident that we have no case of this kind here. Of the two versions, the former is more poetical ; the latter more in earnest. Tottel's version is more exact in its expression. " To get some peace *or* truce " is more correctly put than " to get peace *and* truce." " *Given* you my heart " is far more forcible than "*proffered*." " If *you* it chase, that it in you can find," better serves the unity of the poem than the repetition of the idea of a two-sided persecution implied in " If *I* then it chase," etc.

Moreover, the version given in the Miscellany corrects certain obvious faults in the other. The change made in v. 4 is solely for the purpose of ridding the line of a superfluous syllable. With the alteration from *I* to *you* in v. 9, a similar omission of a superfluous syllable occurs. In no instance do we notice a variation which suggests a blunder in the interpretation or the copying. The order in v. 7 has been changed apparently for no other reason than to avoid the " that that " of the MS. version. With the exception of the omission of a word in v. 4, 9, respectively, all the changes have been made solely as a matter of taste ; nor are they such as would suggest themselves readily to any person other than the poet himself. It is not necessary to suppose that the two versions represent the work of one and the same period ; on the contrary, an interval of several years may have elapsed, and the Italian original of the poem have passed quite out of the writer's mind.

This brief presentation of these two poems may be sufficient to illustrate the possible results of a critical examination of the two texts. In some instances Tottel's reading will be found corrupt ; in other cases, to all appearance, a later version from the poet's own hand. From a comparison of the texts as they are available in the editions named, it is unmistakably evident that the Harington text precedes that on which Tottel's reading is based. It remains to be discovered, in the case of each variation for itself, whether the responsibility for the change rests with the poet or with some other.

B. The Interpretation.

In the opening portion of our essay we considered, in so far as we are acquainted with them, the leading events in Wyatt's life. We allowed ourselves, in that discussion, to be confined for our sources of information almost entirely to such records of the time as have come down to us. Scarcely any reference was made to Wyatt as a poet, and almost no attempt to draw further information from his works. It is our purpose now to turn to Wyatt's poems for assistance ; and in their interpretation to seek for some additional light upon the poet's history. The writer hopes to establish the fact that Wyatt's poetry is more completely than supposed the suggestion and expression of his own experience ; and further, that the possibility exists of tracing the development of that experience, and thus arriving at a definite criterion for determining the order, and approximately the date of groups, at least, of the poet's compositions.

It is an easy matter to arrange the activity of the poet in two grand divisions. Alscher, in his work on Wyatt, before referred to, regards the line as falling coincident with the poet's imprisonment on Bonner's charges about the beginning of 1541. For reasons stated in our biographical sketch, an earlier date appears more satisfactory, and we prefer to regard the year 1536 as marking the turning-point in the poet's career. The disturbance in the political world at that time, the events following upon the arraignment of Anne Boleyn, Wyatt's own critical position, appear to have worked profoundly on his mind, and have left an evident impress on his work.

The earlier of the two grand divisions indicated may be called the Court Period of Wyatt's life. It includes the years from 1521 or 1522 to the year 1536, beginning with Wyatt's entrance into public life at seventeen or eighteen years of age. During this period, as we have seen, he visited France with Sir Thomas Cheney in 1526; accompanied Sir John Russell to Italy in 1527; and during the greater part of 1529–1530 was employed as high marshal of Calais. With these interruptions, so far as we can gather from the sources available, Wyatt was prominent among the distinguished gentlemen of Henry's Court, finding leisure now and then to indulge his taste and talent for poetic composition. To this period belong almost all the love-poems, — the sonnets, the rondeaux, many of the epigrams, and nearly all that varied collection of appeals and plaints which he has left us to interpret and to puzzle over, wondering if the poet is to be taken at his word; not always able to discover what he really means.

The characteristics of the works which follow in the second period of Wyatt's activity are especially a deeper insight, a more earnest view of life; the expression of religious feeling; an inclination to philosophize. It is the period of the Satires and the Paraphrase of the Penitential Psalms. We are able also to assign a few scattered sonnets, epigrams, and other poems to this later period; in a few cases to fix the date more accurately.

A word in regard to the principle of interpretation followed. Most of Wyatt's love-poems are nominally addressed to a distinct personality; they pretend to record the poet's own experiences and fortunes. Our only test as to the reliability of this appearance lies in a comparison of the poems among themselves. If we are able to discern resemblances and peculiarities of thought and form, to arrange in groups distinguished by a characteristic principle of treatment, and then to trace a line of unity and an order of development running through them all, we may then seek to reconcile the results of our theoretical arrangement with the known facts in Wyatt's biography, and try to determine the personality of his heroine.

Wyatt's earlier versification was materially different from that which he subsequently adopted; and this fact makes it comparatively easy to select some among his poems which must have been produced at a very early date. Nott, in his essay on the versification of Wyatt, also in his dissertation contained in the volume devoted to Surrey, calls it " rhythmical," " differing in no respect from that of either Hawes or Barclay, or the other writers who preceded him." [1] By the term " rhythmical," Nott means a verse cast not in the regular iambic decasyllabic form, but one read with a strongly marked cæsura in the middle of the line, containing more or fewer syllables than the verses which precede and follow, but agreeing with them in the number of principal accents, generally four, and depending on the use of the pause, and the swing of the verse, for its conformity to the general rhythm. It might happen, and indeed does, that the line is decasyllabic without necessarily becoming iambic also; and here it is necessary to read the verse, not with the accent bestowed as in an iambic line, but in the older style with the cæsura strongly marked and the stress placed on those syllables where it would most naturally fall. The following verses may serve to illustrate the meaning of the paragraph : —

> " But déath were delíverance | and lífe length of páin.
> Of twó ills, let sée, | nów choose the lést.
> This bírd to delíver, | yóu that hear her pláin ;
> Yóur advice, you lóvers, | whích shall be bést ? "
>
> N. 48 ; T. 225 ; A. 55.

We have given Nott's reading of the lines, Tottel's version having been altered so as to conform much more closely to the normal type. Whether the change proceeded from the editor,

---

[1] Essay in the vol. of Wyatt's poems, p. cxlviii; also in the dissertation preceding Surrey's poems, p. clxxxiv.

or from the poet, it is evident that we have the original form before us. An intermediate stage followed this earliest period, characterized by an accurate observance of the French rule regulating the number of syllables in the line. It is for his elevation of this principle, so important in the development of English metre, that Wyatt deserves the highest recognition. But while methodically observant of this rule, Wyatt often failed to reconcile the, at times antagonistic, word-accent and verse-stress. This task fell rather on Surrey's shoulders; while elaborating the principle which Wyatt had established, he succeeded in adapting the foreign verse to English pronunciation, and demonstrated the principle of agreement between the two. The following verses will serve as illustration : —

> " The lóng love thát in mý thought dóth harbóur,
> And ín mine héart doth kéep his résidénce,
> Intó my fáce presséth with bóld preténce,
> And thérein cámpeth spréading hís bannér." [1]
>
> N. 1 ; T. 33 ; A. 1.

It is interesting to compare Surrey's treatment of the metre in his translation of this same sonnet : —

> " Lóve that líveth, and refgneth ín my thoúght,
> That búilt his séat withín my cáptive bréast,
> Cládd in the árms, whereín with mé he foúght,
> Oft ín my fáce he dóth his bánner rést."
>
> Tottel's Misc., p. 8.

From the comparative fewness in examples of the earliest type of verse construction, it is evident that Wyatt very soon passed to this second stage, and that the poems cast in the style of *The long love* are still among the early compositions. The development of Wyatt's system was of course gradual ; hence we find verses characteristic of either period intruding among those which represent another. Having recognized then the gradual development of Wyatt's skill in his progress from

---

[1] Compare Alscher, *Sir Thomas Wyatt, etc.*, Wiener Beiträge, i. 77.

the rougher work of the earliest period to that of the third, the
period of his best and most harmonious work, we are provided
with a means for deciding which among his poems we may call
his earliest; we then pass on to the comparison of the others,
relying on our interpretation of the poems and any chance pe-
culiarity of metre or of form that may distinguish them.   As the
poems are arranged in groups, they will be classified according
to their stanza form ; this plan will enable us to avoid some confusion in determining the relation of the poems to one another
within the groups, and at the same time help us to trace the
prevalence of special forms at particular periods.

EARLIEST POEMS.

		N. .	T.	A.
Sonnets.	Avising the bright beams	10	40	11
	Ever mine hap is slack	12	68	13
	Love and Fortúne and my	12	69	13
	Like to these unmeaśurable	13	70	15
Ottava Rima.	For shamefast harm	65	82	165
	Vulcan begat me	65	82	166
Rhyme Royal.	Like as the bird	47	225	54
a b a b	Absence absenting	258	—	142

It is probable that Wyatt had written poems earlier than those
which compose this group, but these bear all the marks of
apprenticeship, and are to be designated as his earliest work
that has come down to us.   The metre here employed is that
which has been already described as characteristic of the earliest
compositions.   The pieces may be characterized collectively as
crude.   They are almost without exception drawn from foreign
sources.   *Avising the bright beams* is probably a translation,
the first word of the sonnet being used evidently in the sense
of the Italian *avvissare*, "to look at attentively."[1]   It seems
likely that the word was suggested to the poet by the presence

---

[1] Nott, Notes, p. 541.

of the Italian word in the original of what we here conjecture to be a translation merely. We find another example similar to this in the sonnet *If amorous faith.*[1] V. 5 reads in Nott's version, " If in my visage each thought *depainted.*" *Depainted* is not a common word ; and in the Miscellany the word *distained* is substituted ; but the MS. reading is correct, and was suggested by the Italian word *dipinto,* which occurs in the original. *Ever mine hap is slack* is a translation of Petrarch's 44th sonnet : *Mie venture al venir son tarde e pigre.* *Love and Fortune* is from Petrarch's 99th sonnet : *Amor, Fortuna, e la mia mente schiva.* *Like to these,* was stated by Puttenham to be a translation of one of Petrarch's sonnets also ; Nott believes this to be a mistake, but thinks it was probably borrowed from some Italian writer of the school of Tibaldeo or Accolti.[2] *For shamefast harm* is paraphrased from the epigram of Ausonius : *Thesauro invento qui limina mortis inibat.*[3] *Vulcan begat me* occurs in the MS. with this title : " A riddle *ex Pandulpho.*" The original begins, *Vulcanus genuit; peperit Natura.*[4] *Like as the bird,* and *Absence absenting,* are, so far as we know, original poems. As regards the interpretation of these early poems, little need be said. The sonnets are translations, and probably nothing more. *Avising the bright beams* may be addressed to some particular lady ; the others probably not. *Like as the bird* and the two epigrams are of course mere exercises of skill or pleasure. *Absence absenting* perhaps refers to some period of absence from Court, but is to be regarded as a message of gallantry rather than the utterance of a real passion. It is to be noted that among what seem to be the earliest of Wyatt's compositions, we find the sonnet, the rhyme royal stanza, familiar through the use made of it by Chaucer, the *ottava rima,* like the sonnet, borrowed from his Italian masters, and the simple cross rhyme *a b a b.* We find no example of the single rhyme stanza in the group.

[1] N. 14; T. 70; A. 15.
[2] Nott, Notes, p. 543.
[3] Nott, p. 554.
[4] Nott, p. 555.

GROUP I. OF THE LOVE-POEMS.

a. *Sonnets.*

	N.	T.	A.
The long love	1	33	1
The lively sparks	3	34	3
Such vain thought	4	35	4
Unstable dream	4	35	4
[Cæsar, when that	6	37	6]
[Each man tells me	7	37	7]
Some fowls there be	7	38	8
Because I have	8	38	8
I find no peace	9	39	9
My galley charged	9	39	10
Such is the course	11	62	12
If amorous faith	14	70	15

The two sonnets in brackets are placed rather doubtfully in this group; perhaps they might with equal, or better, propriety be assigned to the earliest period. Aside from this there is apparent connection between the poems of the set. The following are from Petrarch : —

1. The long love.	*Amor, che nel pensier.*
2. Such vain thought.	*Pien d'un vago pensier.*
3. Cæsar, when that.	*Cesare, poi che 'l traditor.*
4. Some fowls there be.	*Son animali al mondo.*
5. Because I have thee.	*Perch' io t'abbia guardato.*
6. I find no peace.	*Pace non trovo.*
7. My galley charged.	*Passa la nave mia.*
8. If amorous faith.	*S'una fede amorosa.*

All of these Italian originals may be found in the notes to Nott's edition, No. 5 excepted. It is seen that a large proportion of this group also is translation ; and it must be added that the opening verse of *The lively sparks* is borrowed from Petrarch as well, the original being found in Petrarch's 220th sonnet, *Vive faville uscian de' duo bei lumi.*

In versification these poems are about on a level. The verses are pretty generally in the style of what in a preceding paragraph we termed the second stage of Wyatt's art; still, the quicker-moving four-stress verse recurs often, and almost every sonnet of the number contains examples. Let it be said in this connection that it is to the reading as given by the Harington MS. text that we must look for the original form in which these poems appeared; and it is naturally the original appearance of the poem only that can be of any value here. Not only do we note an improvement in versification in passing from the last group to that now before us, but we notice also that there is more of poetry in the thought, and greater ease and vigor in expression. The facility and regularity of a later period are still wanting, but it is evident that we here have other than mere beginnings. The sentiment is the same in all; and the question of the interpretation of the poems naturally arises. Perhaps it will be best to leave this question until we have examined the remaining poems to be assigned to the group.

b. *Rhyme-royal Stanza.*

		N.	T.	A.
Thou restful place	. . . . . .	24	45	33
Resound my voice	. . . . .	25	43	34
For want of will	. . . . . .	36	59	44
What word is that	. . . . .	80	223	183

The reader will not fail to note the strong resemblance in the poems here presented; not only in stanza form, and in the thought embodied in that form, but in the style of expression and the general effect of the individual poems, there is unanimity so marked as to indicate the work of a single period.

Thou restful place and *Resound my voice* are very closely related, and both are suggestive of the sonnet *Unstable dream.*[1] In the concluding stanza of *Resound my voice* we find these verses : —

[1] N. 4; T. 35; A. 4.

> " Why then, alas, doth not she on me *rue ?*
> Or is her heart so hard that no pity
> May in it sink, *my joy for to renew ?* "

This is helpful in a double way : it sustains the correctness of Nott's reading in his version of the sonnet *Unstable dream,* v. 6, 7 : —

> " By tasted sweetness make me not to *rue*
>
> .   .   .   .
>
> .   .   .   .
>
> Thou broughtest not her into this tossing mew ;
> But madest my sprite live *my care to renew."*

Wyatt was somewhat restricted in his rhymes, and the same rhyme frequently recurs in his poems, especially in those of a single period. The occurrence of this rhyme here, therefore, not only attests the accuracy of the MS. text ; it also emphasizes the probability that both poems are productions of about the same date.

For want of will introduces an eight-syllable iambic verse which is employed with great perfection throughout ; not a single irregularity occurring within its lines. This poem is found in Tottel only ; hence we are not certain that it is the original form of the poem which we now have before us. It has all the appearance of a real love-poem ; it is not a translation nor an imitation, so far as known, but an original production, inspired by genuine feeling.

What word is that ? also in eight-syllable verse ; and here again the measure is employed with complete success. The MS. text varies somewhat from that used by Tottel, and in this case the reading of the latter version seems more characteristic of the poet than does the former. The closing verse,

> "It is my *salve.*and eke my *sore,"*

has its parallel in the two following lines : —

> " Why dost thou stick to *salve* that thou madest *sore ?* "[1]
> "My gain, my loss, my *salve,* my *sore."*[2]

[1] N. 71, 4 ; A. 172, 12 ; T. 66, 18.   [2] N. 27, 22 ; A. 36, 15 ; T. 52, 18.

There can be no doubt that in this case the poet is addressing his lines to a particular lady. The epigram is introduced among the poems of this group, not for the purpose of giving a personal color to the romance developing, but because, as will be seen with our progress, there is no appropriate place for it among the groups which follow.

c. *Ottava Rima.*

	N.	T.	A.
The furious gun	70	54	171

This epigram naturally belongs with the *early* poems of this group, — with the sonnets which are marked by the same irregularity in metre. It is like most of them, a translation or imitation of an Italian original, being borrowed from the poet Serafino.

d. *a b a b Stanza.*

	N.	T.	A.
So unwarely	39	65	47
Comfort thyself	166	—	70
Heaven and earth	154	—	58
Process of time	185	—	86
Like as the swan	187	—	87
Like as the wind	—	—	184

So unwarely contains suggestions of both Petrarch and Chaucer; v. 5, for instance, is perhaps a repetition of—

> " But I was hurt right now thorough mine eye
> Into mine heart."[1]

And the line *Down unto my heart it ran,* was perhaps suggested by the verse in one of Petrarch's sonnets : —

> " *Ed aperta la via per gli occhi al core.*"[2]

The third stanza of this poem repeats the thought of the son-

---

[1] *Cant. Tales,* l. 1099.   [2] Nott, p. 549.

net *Some fowls there be*.[1] This piece introduces a novelty in
its manner of construction ; while the first three verses of every
stanza are decasyllables, the stanza closes in each instance with
an octosyllabic verse.

Comfort thyself is evidently expressive of the writer's real
feelings. He indicates the despair into which he has fallen :
to speak is useless ; but the yoke is on his neck, and he cannot shake it off. This poem is entirely in eight-syllable verse.

Heaven and earth, in its general style, suggests a possible
connection with *Resound my voice*.[2] It evidently belongs with
the latest poems of this period : —

> " It is not now, but long and long ago
> I have you served, — " (v. 7.)

Process of time. This poem is written in a peculiar measure ;
the presence of irregularly recurring anapæstic feet produces a
singular rhythmical effect, and yet the result is not unpleasing,
nor can we regard this peculiar metre a characteristic of Wyatt's
earliest period alone, — indeed we find pieces of this character
at a time presumably much later than this. Of the relation between this poem and the others in the set we shall soon have
better opportunity to speak.

Like as the swan is in import similar to *Heaven and earth*.
We here have a complete verse serving as refrain, and suggestive, in its repetition, of the plan followed in that poem.

Like as the wind : not found in Nott's edition. It voices
the same complaints as the preceding poems. In the next to
the closing stanza there again seems to be a reference to *Some
fowls there be :*[3] —

> " Like as the fly doth seek the flame,
> And afterward playeth in the fire,
> Who findeth her woe, and seeketh her game,
> Whose grief doth grow of her own desire."

---

[1] N. 7 ; T. 38 ; A. 8.   [2] N. 25 ; T. 43 ; A. 34.   [3] N. 7 ; T. 38 ; A. 8.

e. *Single-Rhyme Stanza.*

With the advent of this period Wyatt begins to employ the single-rhyme stanza, but in connection with a short refrain, which may or may not rhyme with the verses which precede. The eight-syllable verse prevails; the stanzas consist sometimes of three, sometimes of four lines. We group the following here: —

	N.	T.	A.
What meaneth this	215	—	105
To cause accord	179	—	80
To wish and want	173	—	75
What rage is this	45	80	52

What meaneth this. There is evidently connection between this poem and two already mentioned, — *Unstable dream*[1] and *Thou restful place.*[2] All three poems derive their motive from a common source; and the reader may make an interesting comparison if he chooses, by turning to our English translation, the "Romaunt of the Rose," beginning with v. 2525. The sixth and seventh stanzas, too, —

> "But if I sit near her by,
> With loud voice my heart doth cry,
> And yet my mouth is dumb and dry;
> What means this?

> "To ask for help no heart I have;
> My tongue doth fail what I should crave;
> Yet inwardly I rage and rave:
> What means this?" —

contain suggestions of the sonnet *Because I have thee.*[3]

To cause accord and *To wish and want* contain allusions obviously suggestive of the sentiments and expressions found in other poems of this set, and seem to find their appropriate place in the group.

---

[1] N. 4; T. 35; A. 4.   [2] N. 24; T. 45; A. 33.   [3] N. 8; T. 38; A. 8.

What rage is this differs from the three poems which precede, in that the measure is decasyllabic, and the short verse
taking the place of the refrain is a simple six-syllable line not
rhyming with the others in the stanza, nor having connection
in any way with the corresponding verse in the other stanzas.
The poem will be referred to later.

f. *Anomalous Forms.*

There are several other poems which are grouped most appropriately with the foregoing. The stanza form differs here ;
and as the pieces are not to be classified under any of the types
already noted, and to increase the number of subordinate
classes might prove confusing on account of the great variety
of rhyme combinations, we allow these anomalous forms to con-
stitute a class by themselves. They appear to have generated
spontaneously with Wyatt, and in many cases are employed in
only a single composition.

	N.	T.	A.
My love is like	232	—	120
At last withdraw	209	—	100
Heart oppressed	227	—	116
Love doth again	253	—	139
Since ye delight	169	—	72
Sufficed not	78	76	180
Lo how I seek	231	—	119
Pass forth	32	56	40

Without stopping for further comment upon the sentiment of
these poems, the connection and the application of which is
sufficiently obvious, we will point out the peculiarities of construction which are their principal characteristic.

My love is like : a b a b c c c d d.

At last withdraw : a b a b c c d d d.

It is interesting here to note the similarity in the rhyme
order, — probably one suggested the other. In the first case,

however, the verse is decasyllabic throughout ; while.in the last named, the stanza is metabolic : the two *a* rhymes being eight-syllable ; the others six-syllable.

Heart oppressed : a b a b c c.

The verse is eight-syllable. This simple stanza-form, occurring quite often in Wyatt's poetry, might have been a development of the rhyme royal stanza *a b a b* [*b*] *c c*, or of the *ottava rima, a b a b* [*a b*] *c c.*

Love doth again : a a b a a b.

Here we have the so-called " tail-rhyme " stanza. It is the first example which we have found of the use of the *short line* by Wyatt. The *a* verses are dipodies, the *b* six-syllable. It is possible to regard such a combination as a dismembered fourteen-syllable verse ; but it is improbable that Wyatt had this origin in mind.

Since ye delight : a a b b a a + r.

In this poem the two *b* verses are each of four syllables ; the *a* lines trimeter, and the refrain eight-syllable.

Sufficed not : a b b a.

The verse is pentameter throughout.

Lo how I seek : a b a b b c b c.

This poem is entirely in eight-syllable verse.

Pass forth : a b a b c d c d.

The poem is composed in six-syllable verse ; the stanza form is very similar to the last. One might be disposed to consider this a simple *a b a b* stanza ; but the division is made with reference to the thought as well as to the rhyme, each octavo treating of a particular motive and being complete in itself. In connection with this poem we desire to examine three other pieces, already noted, which stand in close connection with it and with one another. These are : *Such is the course* (class *a*), *Process of time* (class *d*), and *What rage is this* (class *e*). When these four poems are compared, their mutual relation is obvious.

Pass forth (N. 32 ; T. 56 ; A. 40).
v. 17-24.

"And as the water soft,
Without forcing or strength,
Where that it falleth oft
Hard stones doth pierce at
    length :
So in her stony heart
My plaints at last shall grave,
And, rigour set apart,
Win grant of that I crave."

Process of time (N. 185 ;
A. 86).

"Process of time worketh such
    wonder,
That water which is of kind
    so soft,
Doth pierce the marble stone
    asunder,
By little drops falling from
    aloft.
And yet a heart that seems so
    tender,
Receiveth no drop of the still-
    ing tears
That alway still cause me to
    render
The vain plaint that sounds
    not in her ears."

Such is the course (N. 11 ; T.
62 ; A. 12).

"Such is the course that
    nature's kind hath wrought,
That snakes have time
    to cast away their stings :
Against chain'd prisoners
    what need defence be sought?
The fierce lion will hurt
    no yielden things."

Ditto, v. 9-12 ; 17-20.

"So cruel, alas ! is naught alive,
So fierce, so froward, so out of
    frame,
But some way, some time may
    so contrive
By means the wild to temper
    and tame.

.   .   .   .   . .

The lion in his raging furour
Forbears that sueth, meekness
    for his boot ;
And thou, alas ! in extreme
    dolour,
The heart so low thou treads
    under thy foot."

Pass forth, v. 9-12.	*Ditto*, v. 13-16.
" For though hard rocks among She seems to have been bred, And of the tiger long Been nourished and fed."	"And I that always have sought, and seek Each place, each time for some lucky day, This fierce tiger, less I find her meek, And more denied the longer I pray."

What rage is this (N. 45 ; T. 80 ; A. 52).
v. 11-16.

" Go to, triumph, rejoice thy goodly turn,
  Thy friend thou dost oppress.
Oppress thou dost, and hast of him no cure,
Nor yet my plaint no pity can procure,
Fierce tiger fell ! hard rock without recure !
  Cruel rebel to love ! "

It must be agreed that the similarity in motive and expression noted in the case of these four poems is quite remarkable. Such correspondence is more than unusual in works separated by long intervals in time of composition ; and in the absence of any evidence pointing to the contrary, we may feel entirely justified in referring the pieces cited to a common date.

This brings us to the end of the list of compositions assigned to this group. We have tried to show the existence of an intimate relationship among them ; but the demonstration of this relationship must be sought in a study of the poems named. It is impossible to do more than barely indicate superficial resemblances here ; the strongest evidence, after all, is found in the general impression resulting from a comprehensive survey of the entire field. Similarity of sentiment, the frequent recurrence of a favorite motive, the repetition of characteristic forms of expression, would seem to indicate that the poems thus related must be the productions of a single period. Of the poems here collected, the sonnets were probably among the earliest compositions. Those cast in other forms of verse arrangement show for the most part a higher development of art and skill. Moreover, as we advance we note the growing infrequency of translations; the percentage of poems from a foreign source is very high among the earliest pieces. The original poems have all the appearance of being the expression of real feelings and experiences; the thoughts uttered in these pieces are taken up and repeated in the translated poems : we therefore judge that the pieces chosen for translation were selected with regard to their contents. Our plan of grouping can be judged upon its merits only after the various groups have been presented and the order of growth established.

This early period may be designated as that of Protestation and Entreaty; a new motive is introduced in the group to follow.

GROUP I. OF THE LOVE-POEMS.

SONNETS.	N.	T.	A.
The long love . . .	1	33	1
The lively sparks . .	3	34	3
Such vain thought .	4	35	4
Unstable dream . .	4	35	4
[Cæsar when that .	6	37	6]
[Each man tells me .	7	37	7]
Some fowls there be .	7	38	8
Because I have . .	8	38	8
I find no peace . .	9	39	9
My galley charged .	9	39	10
Such is the course .	11	62	12
If amorous faith .	14	70	15

OTTAVA RIMA.	N.	T.	A.
The furious gun	70	54	171

SINGLE-RHYME.	N.	T.	A.
What meaneth this .	215	—	105
To cause accord . .	179	—	80
To wish and want .	173	—	75
What rage is this .	45	80	52

RHYME ROYAL.	N.	T.	A.
Thou restful place .	24	45	33
Resound my voice .	25	43	34
For want of will. .	36	59	44
What word is that .	80	223	183

ANOMALOUS.	N.	T.	A.
My love is like . .	232	—	120
At last withdraw .	209	—	100
Heart oppressed .	227	—	116
Love doth again .	253	—	139
Since ye delight .	169	—	72
Sufficed not . .	78	76	180
Lo how I seek . .	231	—	119
Pass forth my . .	32	56	40

a b a b STANZA.	N.	T.	A.
So unwarely . .	39	65	47
Comfort thyself .	166	—	70
Heaven and earth .	154	—	58
Process of time .	185	—	86
Like as the swan .	187	—	87
Like as the wind .	—	—	184

6

GROUP II.

We enter herewith upon a second phase of the poet's verse. In the compositions of this period the lover expresses himself as happy in the love of his lady, but forever harassed by necessity of concealment; the affection is mutual, but disclosure of the relationship would be fatal to the happiness of both. This motive binds the group of poems unmistakably together, strongly attests the fact that here is the record of a real experience, and casts a most important light upon the personality of the heroine. At this time Wyatt does not appear to have turned to the sonnet as the form selected to express his fancies, nor to the stanza made familiar by Chaucer's use of it. The lighter cross-rhyme stanza, and the short, crisp form of the epigram, appear to be the favorite types of the group. We have : —

a. *a b a b Stanza.*

	N.	T.	A.
Once, as methought	21	63	30
After great storms	156	—	60
I love, loved.	211	—	102
The heart and service	214	—	104

The idea of concealment does not appear in the first two poems mentioned; these serve as an introduction to this stage in the romance, and are devoted to rejoicings at the good fortune which the lover now enjoys. The connection between the two poems is obvious : —

Once, as methought (v. 9–16).   *After great storms* (v. 1–8).

" Yet for all that a stormy blast   " After great storms the calm
Had overturned this goodly day;   returns,
And Fortune seemed at the last   And pleasanter it is thereby;
That to her promise she said nay.   Fortune likewise that often turns,
                                                              Hath made me now the most
                                                              happy.

But like as one out of despair,
To sudden hope revived I;
Now Fortune sheweth herself so fair,   .
That I content me wondrously."

The Heaven that pitied my distress,
My just desire, and my cry;
Hath made my languor to cease,
And me also the most happy."

In the former of the two poems we are further told : —

> " My most desire my hand may reach,
> My will is alway at my hand;
> Me need not long for to beseech
> Her that hath power me to command.
>
> What earthly thing more can I crave ?
> What would I wish more at my will ?
> Nothing on earth more would I have,
> Save that I have, to have it still."

I love, loved, introduces us suddenly to the peculiar circumstances in which the lovers are placed : —

> " O ! deadly yea !   O ! grievous smart !
> Worse than refuse, unhappy gain !
> In love who ever play'd this part,
> To love so well, and live in pain.
>
> Were ever hearts so well agreed,
> Since love was love, as I do trow,
> That in their love so evil did speed,
> To love so well, and live in woe."

The last stanza of the poem hints at reasons why the course of this true love runs so roughly ; we shall find similar allusions in other poems to certain individuals, " that causers be of this," and who have it in their power to interrupt the happiness of the pair, and apparently to bring them into peril.

The heart and service. In this poem the tone is somewhat changed. One might think the lady had become coquettish, as the lover seems protesting to a degree. Still, he declares hopefully : —

> " Do which you list, I shall not want
> To be your servant *secretly*."

b. *Anomalous Forms.*

	N.	A.
Such hap as I	171	73
To seek each where	152	56

Such hap as I depicts the lover in the same predicament as before described.   In the third stanza the lover laments, —

> " For though I have, such is my lot,
> In hand to help that I require,
> It helpeth not."

This seems like a recollection of

> " My most desire my·hand may reach,
> My will is alway at my hand."
>   N. 22, 13 ; A. 31, 13.

In

> " To ask and have, and yet therefore
> Refrain I must,"

the lover expresses plainly the hard circumstances of his case ; in subsequent poems the declaration is justified.

The form of this poem is quite peculiar ; the rhyme-order, *a b a b c b c*, might be considered almost as an attempt to introduce a *terzine* stanza.   The lines are octosyllabic, with the exception of the last verse, which is four-syllable ; this concluding half-verse becomes in each case the introductory half-verse of the following stanza.

To seek each where was probably written about the same time as *The heart and service* (N. 214 ; A. 104).   It was evidently a New Year's greeting from the lover to his lady.   The poem has the rhyme-order, *a a b a b b;* all except the closing couplet is in octosyllabic verse ; these last two verses are decasyllables.

c. *Single-rhyme Stanza.*

	N.	A.
Take heed by time	208	99
Sometime I sigh . ·	223	112
[I am as I am	262	147]

Take heed by time is a merry warning to his lady, lest she on her side betray the affection which they wish to conceal.

> " If they might take you in that trap,
> They would soon leave it in your lap;
> To love unspied is but a hap;
> Therefore, take heed ! "

The form of this poem corresponds exactly to that of *What meaneth this !* (N. 215 ; A. 105.) *Sometime I sigh* continues to express the sentiment appropriate to this period. Still, the piece denotes some progress towards a time of uncertainty and doubt regarding the lady's attitude in the affair. There is a suggestiveness of *The heart and service* about the poem.

The heart and service (N. 214; A. 104).	*Sometime I sigh* (v. 17-20).
"The heart and service to you proffered	" All my poor heart, and my love true,
With right good will full honestly,	While life doth last, I give it you;
Refuse it not since it is offered,	And you to serve with service due,
But take it to you gentlely.	And never to change you for no new.
(v. 17-20.)	**(v. 13-16.)**
Pain or pleasure now may you plant,	When ye be merry why should I care ?
Even which it please you stead-fastly ;	Ye are my joy and my welfare,
Do which you list, I shall not want	I will you love, I will not spare
To be your servant secretly."	Into your presence, as far as I dare."

This poem is one of those before alluded to cast in the peculiar style of *Process of Time* (N. 185 ; A. 86). The verses should be scanned in accordance with the principle mentioned in a paragraph introductory to this section of our work, *e. g.* :

" Sómetime I sígh,   sómetime I síng ;
Sómetime I laúgh,   sómetime mourníng
As óne in doúbt,   this ís my sayíng
Have I' displeásed you   in ány thíng ? "

I am as I am is of precisely similar character. There is so
little in this poem significant for our purpose that we are doubtful where it really should be placed. It suggests somewhat the
sonnets, *Cæsar, when that the traitor of Egypt* (N. 6 ; T. 37 ;
A. 6), and *Each man tells me* (N. 7 ; T. 37 ; A. 7). This
composition is, however, so superior to the two sonnets in its easy
fluency compared with the laborious awkwardness of their style,
as to suggest strongly its belonging to a later date. On account
of its exact correspondence in form to the poem just examined,
and because of the fact that it contains nothing contrary to the
general sentiment of the group, the poem is inserted here.

d. *Ottava Rima.*

	N.	T.	A.
The fruit of all	236	—	124
Of purpose Love	64	80	164
Alas ! Madam	66	41	167
The wand'ring gadling	6/	41	167
What needeth these	67	42	168
She sat and sewed	69	52	170
Who hath heard	69	52	170
Nature that gave	70	65	172
All in thy look	71	66	172
Th' en'my of life	67	63	168

This collection of epigrams has been here introduced as very
probably of this period. The first and last named of the series
may safely be assigned to it ; but the others are of such a nature
that it is impossible to speak with certainty about them. If not
here, they belong to a quite later period ; but the probability is
that they find their proper place within this group.

The fruit of all is certainly a production of the date represented in *Such hap as I* (N. 171 ; A. 73).

The fruit of all (v. 1, 2).

" The fruit of all the service that
    I serve
Despair doth reap; such hapless
    hap have I.

Such hap as I (v. 34, 35).

" With hapless hand no man hath
    raught
    Such hap as I."

(v. 3, 4.)

But though he have no power to
    make me swerve,
Yet by the fire for cold I feel I
    die.

(v. 17, 18.)

And still of cold I me bewail,

And rakèd am in burning fire.

(v. 5, 6.)

In paradise for hunger still I
    sterve,
And in the flood for thirst to
    death I dry;

(v. 11, 12.)

That know I not, unless I sterve,

For hunger still amiddes my
    food.

(v. 7, 8.)

So Tantalus am I, and in worse
    pain,
Amidst my help that helpless
    doth remain."

(v. 19–21.)

For though I have, such is my
    lot,
In hand to help that I require,
    It helpeth not."

Of purpose Love is a pretty, affectionate conceit, easily ima-
gined to be a product of this time.

The wand'ring gadling introduces perhaps the figure of a
rival to our notice.

Alas! Madam and *What needeth these* are translations from
the Italian of Serafino; the originals, *Incolpa, Donna, amor se
troppo io volsi* and *A che minacci! a che tanta ira e orgoglio!*
are given entire by Nott (p. 555).

She sat and sewed and *Who hath heard* refer to one event;
they may be humorous, satirical complaints of the coquetry of
his lady-love, or, together with the two just preceding, may be
the light and fanciful productions of a later day.

Nature that gave is inserted in this group with more confidence than in any other.

All in thy look might possibly be assigned to an earlier date ; but it is allowed to remain with the rest.

Th' en'my of life. For the suggestion of this poem we have to look to the days of Chaucer and his imitators ; and once more we find the motive in a passage of the " Romaunt of the Rose." With verse 1715 of that work the translator introduces the episode of the attempt to seize the rose in the garden. The lover approaches to grasp the bud·whose beauty has aroused his desire, but Love stands ready with his shafts, and shoots first one, and then another, and another ; all his arrows taking effect upon the trespasser. In verse 1878 and following, the poet describes how Love at last takes an arrow, *Fairesemblaunt,* the head of which was anointed with a precious ointment : —

(v. 1890.) " Somdelle to yeve a-leggement
Upon the woundes that he hadde
Thurgh the body in my herte made,
To helpe her sores, and to cure,
And that they may the bette endure.
But yit this arwe, withoute more,
Made in myn herte a large sore
That in fulle grete peyne I abode.
But ay the oynement wente abrode ;
Thourgh-oute my woundes large and wide,
It spredde aboute in every side ;
Thorough whos vertu and whos myght
Myn herte joyfulle was and light."

This, I take it, suggested the idea of the epigram. But we must still supply an interpretation of it. Who is the " enemy " referred to ? It cannot be Love, for Love does not wither away the green with his cold ; moreover, Love is mentioned in the closing lines as quite distinct from the enemy who has shot this arrow at the lover. The early editor interprets the enemy to be Deadly Sickness ; perhaps this explanation is allowable, but it is not very suggestive. How deadly sickness can aggravate a wound of this kind is not clear. I would suggest that the enemy is Jealousy. He certainly deserves the bad character given him in the first two lines; he might, very plausibly too, suggest to the lover his ability to rid him of his smart; and the issue of this course of treatment, increasing rather than lessening the lover's affection and his pain, is certainly a possible and a poetical result. Whichever interpretation is to be preferred, the poem falls most naturally in this group.

This brings us to the end of our second period; it may be called, perhaps, the period of Prosperity or Attainment. From this point the lover's star begins to descend.

GROUP II. OF THE LOVE-POEMS.

a b a b STANZA.	N.	T.	A.	OTTAVA RIMA.	N.	T.	A.	ANOMALOUS.	N.	T.	A.
Once, as methought	21	63	30	The fruit of all	236	—	124	Such hap as I	171	—	73
After great storms	156	—	60	Of purpose Love	64	80	164	To seek each	152	—	56
I love, loved	211	—	102	Alas! Madam	66	41	167				
The heart and service	214	—	104	The wand'ring	67	41	167	SINGLE-RHYME.			
				What needeth	67	42	168				
				She sat and sewed	69	52	170				
				Who hath heard	69	52	170	Take heed by time	208	—	99
				Nature that gave	70	65	172	Sometime I sigh	223	—	112
				All in thy look	71	66	172	[I am as I am	262	—	147]
				Th' en'my of life	67	63	168				

GROUP III.

Introductory to the poems of this general group we find a few in which the lover seems attempting to clear himself of certain accusations brought against him by his mistress. He protests his loyalty to her, and denies the truth of the charges. We have eight poems treating of this theme.

a. *Anomalous Forms.*

	N.	T.	A.
The knot which	224	—	113
It was my choice	226	—	114
Accused though I be.	75	55	177
Perdie I said it not	40	66	48
Ye know my heart	237	—	125

The knot which: a b a b a b a.

"The knot which first my heart did strain,
When that your servant I became,
Doth bind me still for to remain,
Always your own as now I am.

.   .   .   .   .

If in my love there be one spot
Of false deceit or doubleness;
Or if I mind to slip this knot
By want of faith or steadfastness
Let all my service be forgot,
And when I would have chief redress,
Esteem me not."

It was my choice: a b a b c b c.

In this poem no allusion is made to any accusations, but the poet speaks as if some cloud had settled on their intercourse. By right his heart should be accepted, for it was a free-will offering. But the lover fears that *fortune*, or *fancy*, will prove more powerful than *truth*, — here used as a synonym for *right*. He

is in a quandary, uncertain to which of the three he shall appeal; at last he decides to trust to *right;* for right never
changes, while *chance* and *fancy* are fickle and unstable.

> " To Fantasy pertains to choose.
> All this I know: for Fantasy
> First unto love did me induce;   \
> But yet I know as steadfastly,
> That if love have no faster knot,
> So nice a choice slips suddenly.
>   It lasteth not."

Accused though I be: a b a b a b a b a b c c.

Here the lover speaks more plainly of the cause of his lady's
coolness : " ill tongues " have been attacking him.

> " None is alive that can ill tongues eschew ;
> Hold them as false ; and let not us depart
> Our friendship old in hope of any new."

Perdie I said it not: a b a b a c a c.

The protestation is continued. Here the alleged offence is
materialized into the use of some expression, or the utterance
of certain words falsely charged upon the lover. He denies
the slander, and invokes all kinds of misfortune on himself if he
speaks falsely.

> "Perdie I said it not;
> Nor never thought to do:
> As well as I, ye wot,
> I have no power thereto.
> And if I did, the lot,
> That first did me enchain,
> May never slake the knot,
> But straight it to my pain !"

In the fifth stanza he hints that possibly the lady has an
object in her obstinate refusal to credit his assurances, and
queries whether or no this thing be sought to give him pain.

> " If I be clear from thought,
> Why do you then complain?
> Then is this thing but sought
> To turn my heart to pain."

The poem closes with an allusion too dark to be explained by us. Evidently there is another lady in the case, of whom the " Rachel," his true mistress, is, or has pretended to be, jealous. Who " Leah " was, we do not know; nor does " Rachel," in this poem at least, reveal more of her identity.

Ye know my heart: a b a b b c a d e d e c c.

> " Ye know my heart, my Lady dear!
> That since the time I was your thrall
> I have been yours both whole and clear,
> Though my reward hath been but small;
> So am I yet, and more than all.
>
> . . . . .
>
> Ye know also, though ye say nay, ⁃
> That you alone are my desire;
> And you alone it is that may
> Assuage my fervent flaming fire.
>
> . . . . .
>
> And I know well how scornfully
> Ye have mistaken my true intent;
> And hitherto how wrongfully,
> I have found cause for to repent.
> But if your heart doth not relent,
> Since I do know that this ye know,
> Ye shall slay me all wilfully.
>
> . . . . .
>
> Why are ye then so cruel foe
> Unto your own, that loves you so? "

b. *a b a b Stanza.*

	N.	T.	A.
Disdain me not	35	58	43
If Fancy would	161	—	65
I have sought long	172	—	74

Disdain me not repeats the ideas already met.

> " Refuse me not without cause why,
>   Nor think me not to be unjust;
>   Since that by lot of fantasy,
>   This careful knot needs knit I must.
>   Mistrust me not, though some there be
>   That fain would spot my steadfastness :
>   Believe them not, since that ye see
>   The proof is not, as they express."

If Fancy would suggests the thought in *It was my choice* (N. 226 ; A. 114).

If Fancy would (v. 9-18).	*It was my choice* (v. 19-30).
" Fancy doth know how	" Yet some would say assuredly
To further my true heart;	Thou mayst appeal for thy release
If Fancy might avow	To Fantasy.
With Faith to take part.	To Fantasy pertains to choose.
	All this I know : for Fantasy
But Fancy is so frail	First unto love did me induce ;
And flitting still so fast,	But yet I know as steadfastly,
That Faith may not prevail	That if love have no faster knot,
To help me, first nor last.	So nice a choice slips suddenly ;
	It lasteth not.
For Fancy at his lust,	It lasteth not, that stands by
Doth rule all but by guess."	change ;
	Fancy doth change ; Fortune is
	frail."

I have sought long brings us to a turning-point in the lover's experience. His theme is still the changeableness of the lady's fancy ; she has no better reason for her conduct than the man in the proverb : "I reck not how." But the lover's tone has changed.

> " Therefore I played the fool in vain,
>   With pity when I first began
>   Your cruel heart for to constrain,
>   Since love regardeth no doubtful man.
>   But of your goodness, all your mind

Is that I should complain in vain;
This is the favour that I find;
Ye list to hear how I can plain!
    But tho' I plain to please your heart,
Trust me I trust to temper it so,
Not for to care which do revert;
All shall be one, or wealth, or woe.
    For Fancy ruleth, though Right say nay,
Even as the good man kist his cow:
None other reason can ye lay,
But as who sayeth: 'I reck not how.'"

The poems just examined have introduced us to the spirit and sentiment of this period; we now take up the remaining works in turn.

c. *Sonnets.*

	N.	T.	A.
I abide and abide	144	—	20
Though I myself	145	—	21
How oft have I	13	69	14
Was I never yet	2	33	2

I abide and abide. In this sonnet Wyatt returns to the peculiar style of versification found in *Sometime I sigh; I am as I am*, and a few more of the kind already examined by us. The lover becomes impatient at his lady's coldness; she coquets with his devotion, and promises without regard to fulfilment.

    "Much were it better for to be plain,
    Than to say, 'Abide,' and yet not obtain."

Though I myself. The lady has expressed a fear lest she be compelled, against her will, to break the promise given to her lover. The latter chides her for her insincerity, pointing out the fact that all depends upon her own free choice; there is no power can make her change except she give her consent. He says: "I am compelled by force of circumstances to remain inactive under close restraint; everything depends upon yourself. If you seek worldly honor, who can compel you to abide by the

promise made to me? Do not complain, however; nobody
will force you against your will. But I suspect that in spite of
your pretended fear, you are perhaps too ready to listen to the
suit you seem to dread. If really honest, let your defence be
in time, truth, and love; *i. e.*, continue loving and true to me :
time will make all good." Nott says of this difficult poem that
it "is designedly obscure, and probably was never corrected. It
might have been a fine composition. It alludes probably to
Wyatt's unfortunate passion for Anne Boleyn, and intimates that
if she preferred, as she ought to do, honor to ambition, she was
still free to refuse the magnificent proposals which the king
had then laid before her."[1] It seems to me that Nott mis-
interprets the meaning of the third verse; his explanation
contains a contradiction. If the lover means, as Dr. Nott
interprets, " provided you prefer honor to ambition," he would
not ask " who may hold thee to thy promise? " But if he uses
honor in the sense of rank, title, position, there is manifest appropriateness in the question. Dr. Nott would read verses 4, 5,
6, 7, differently; verse 7 thus, —

" Though other present be, I am not all behind."

It would be difficult to justify the change. It seems to me that
the line is particularly keen and forceful as it stands ; it reminds
us of verse 78, in the Third Satire : " Be next thyself . . . "
and means, I think, " You claim to be compelled by another :
I fear you are not altogether opposed to the idea yourself."
The sonnet is indeed obscure ; perhaps we are farther than ever
from the right interpretation. But enough is clear to show that
the sonnet was not written without a purpose. It is not such a
composition as comes from the pen of a mere producer of
society verse. In spite of the obscurity, intensity and directness
characterize it ; and the poem expresses a feeling as real as its
utterance is emphatic. It is to be interpreted in the light of
companion pieces.

[1] Notes, p. 572.

How oft have I contains a sentence of considerable import in verses 3, 4 : —

> ". . . but you do not use
> *Among so high things,* to cast your mind so low."

The original, found, as stated in a previous chapter, among the sonnets of the Italian poet, reads thus : —

> ". . . *M'a voi non piace*
> *Mirar sì basso con la mente altera."*

It will be seen that the slight change in the rendering introduces quite a new thought in the translation. This must have been intended by the poet, and the allusion is evidently to the position or the prospects of the lady thus addressed.

Was I never yet is also a translation of one of Petrarch's sonnets : *Io non fu' d'amar voi lassato unquanco.* This sonnet is very similar in style to the earlier productions of the poet, but because of its agreement with the prevailing sentiment of this period it has been added to the group.

d. *Rhyme-royal Stanza.*

	N.	T.	A.
It may be good	28	42	37
That time that mirth	220	—	109
Though this the port	157	—	61
O miserable sorrow	236	—	124
The joy so short	242	—	129

It may be good. The lover is dissatisfied ; his lady has given many assurances, but he mistrusts her sincerity. He hopes, and yet he dares not hope.

The meaning of the word *hase* in verse 10 is a riddle ; perhaps it was coined as an abbreviation for *hazard,* which would not be inappropriate to the sense.

That time that mirth alludes to the happy days, now past, in which he felt secure in his lady's love. She has now become his " extreme enemy ; " but, —

7

"It is not time that can wear out.
With me, that once is firmly set;
While Nature keeps her course about,
My love from her no man can let.
Though never so sore they me threat,
Yet am I hers, she may be sure ;
And shall be while that life doth dure."

Verse 5 of the stanza quoted is quite significant.
The three remaining poems in this set will be referred to shortly.

e. *Anomalous Forms* (*Second Set*).

	N.	T.	A.
Though I cannot	184	—	85
If with complaint	237	—	125
The answer that	38	62	46
Give place ! all ye	247	—	133
If chance assigned	175	—	77
What death is	180	—	81
Since Love will needs	43	77	51
I see that chance	46	81	53

Though I cannot: a a b b a.

"But I see well, that your high disdain
Will no wise grant that I shall more attain ;
Yet ye must grant at the last
This my poor, and small request;
Rejoice not at my pain ! "

If with complaint: a b a a b b.

"But since it is so far out of measure,
That with my words I can it not contain,
My only trust ! my heart's treasure !
Alas ! why do I still endure
This restless smart and pain ?
Since if ye list ye may my woe restrain."

The answer that: a b a b b.

> " I have no wrong, where I can claim no right,
> Nought ta'en me fro, where I nothing have had:
> Yet of my woe, I cannot so be quite,
> Namely, *Since that another may be glad*
> With that, that thus in sorrow makes me sad.
> Yet none can claim, I say, by former grant,
> That knoweth not of any grant at all;
> And by desert, I dare well make avaunt
> Of faithful will; there is nowhere that shall
> Bear you more truth, more ready at your call."

Give place! all ye: a b a b b b. This piece is somewhat suggestive of *I abide and abide* (N. 144; A. 20).

> " With humble suit I have essayed
> To turn her cruel hearted mind;
> But for reward I am delayed,
> And to my wealth her eyes be blind.
> Lo! thus by chance I am assigned
> With steadfast love to serve the unkind.
>
> .   .   .   .   .   .
>
> For love to find such cruelty,
> Alas! it is a careful lot;
> And for to void such mockery
> There is no way but slip the knot!
> The gain so cold, the pain so hot!
> Praise it who list, I like it not."

If chance assigned: a a a b c c b. An appeal for freedom. The thought expressed in other poems of this group is repeated here; although he dares not hope for favor, the lover remains, nevertheless, bound to her, — he cannot subdue his affection. Now he beseeches that she will give him back his freedom, or else complete his destruction. This fanciful composition may have been suggested by the early poem, *Like as the bird* (N. 47; A. 54).

What death is worse: a b a b b a.   The interpretation of this poem will be considered later.

Since Love will needs: a b a b c c.

> " Though for good-will I find but hate,
>   And cruelly my life to waste,
>   And though that still a wretched state
>   Should pine my days unto the last,
>   Yet I profess it willingly
>   To serve and suffer patiently.
>
> .   .   .   .   .
>
>   Yea ! though Fortune her pleasant face
>   Should shew, to set me up aloft ;
>   And straight my wealth for to deface,
>   Should writhe away, as she doth oft ;   .
>   Yet would I still myself apply
>   To serve and suffer patiently."

I see that chance: a b a b c c.

> " I see that chance hath chosen me
>   Thus *secretly* to live in pain,
>   *And to another* given the fee,
>   Of all my loss to have the gain :
>   By chance assigned thus do I serve,
>   And *other* have that I deserve.
>
> .   .   .   .   .
>
>   To seek by mean to change this mind,
>   Alas ! I prove, it will not be ;
>   For in my heart I cannot find
>   Once to refrain, but still agree,
>   As bound by force, alway to serve,
>   And other have that I deserve."

The reader will not fail to note the close agreement of these two poems, in sentiment as in form ; they belong undoubtedly to a common date, and are assigned with manifest propriety to this third group.

f. *a b a b Stanza* (*Second Set*).

	N.	A.
"Alas! poor man	217	107

> "Alas! poor man, what hap have I,
> *That must forbear that I love best !*
> I trow, it be my destiny,
> Never to live in quiet rest.
>
> .   .   .   .   .
>
> Alas! poor heart, as in this case
> With pensive plaint thou art opprest;
> Unwise thou were *to desire place*
> *Whereas another* is possest.
>
> .   .   .   .   .
>
> She that I serve all other above
> Hath paid my hire, as ye may see;
> I was unhappy, and that I prove,
> To love *above my poor degree.*"

Wyatt's position was not a base one, nor was his family of inferior rank; indeed, there were not many nobles at Henry's Court better situated in this respect than he. This is especially true in reference to the ladies gathered there; and of those to whom Wyatt's address would be most likely paid, there was no one to whom the words here quoted would apply with greater appropriateness than to one exalted not so much by reason of her own connection as by the rank of that person who had displaced the poet in her affections.

g. *Single-Rhyme Stanza.*

	N.	A.
Forget not yet	235	123
And wilt thou	219	108
As power and wit	221	111

Forget not yet.

> "Forget not! oh! forget not this,
> How long ago hath been, and is

The mind that never meant amiss,
      Forget not yet !
Forget not then thine own approved,
The which so long hath thee so loved,
Whose steadfast faith yet never moved :
      Forget not this ! "

And wilt thou leave.

" And wilt thou leave me thus,
  That hath loved thee so long,
  In wealth and woe among ?
  And is thy heart so strong
  As for to leave me thus ?
      Say nay ! say nay !

    .   .   .   .   .

And wilt thou leave me thus,
And have no more pity,
Of him that loveth thee ?
Alas ! thy cruelty !
And wilt thou leave me thus ?
      Say nay ! say nay ! "

As power and wit.

" When all the flock is come and gone
  Mine eye and heart agreeth in one,
  Hath chosen you, only, alone,
  To be my joy, or else my moan,
      Even as ye list.
  Joy, if pity appear in place ;
  Moan, if disdain do shew his face,
  Yet crave I not as in this case,
  But as ye lead to follow the trace,
      Even as ye list.

    .   .   .   .

Dear heart ! I bid your heart farewell,
With better heart than tongue can tell ;
Yet take this tale, as true as gospel,
Ye may my life save or expel
      Even as ye list. "

Similarity in thought, as in expression, characterizes these three poems, and binds them to this group. The general sentiment is this : The lover has served long and faithfully without reward ; but his affection does not falter, he is content to serve even as his lady lists.

h. *Rondeaux.*

Wyatt now turns to the rondeau, — a form borrowed by him from the French, as previously he had borrowed the sonnet from the Italian poets. As belonging distinctively to this period we designate : —

	N.	T.	A.
Behold, Love !	18	53	22
Go ! burning sighs	19	73	24
Help me to seek !	147	—	24
For to love her	148	—	25
If it be so	150	—	27

Behold, Love! In this, as in the poem which follows, *Go! burning sighs*, and in *What 'vaileth truth*, to be discussed hereafter, we must follow the Harington MS. text, which certainly preserves the original form in which these three poems appeared. Their hybrid dress, — half sonnet, half rondeau, — in the version given by Tottel, is not easy of explanation. It is, however, entirely possible that the changed arrangement was the poet's own later work. This does not concern us now, but it is important that we should recognize the form in which the poems were originally composed.

The poem before us declares, —

> " The holy oath whereof she takes no cure,
> Broken she hath."

Furthermore, the lover says, " I am in hold," — which reminds us of the sonnet, *Though I myself be bridled of my mind* (N. 145 ; A. 21).

Go! burning sighs, is an imitation, rather than a translation, of Petrarch's sonnet, *Ite caldi sospiri al freddo core.*

In the latter portion of the poem the thought of the original is entirely lost sight of, — thus showing that Wyatt has here introduced something of his own experience : —

> " I must go work, I see, by craft and art,
> For truth and faith in her is laid apart."

Help me to seek has nothing of special significance for us; its general resemblance to the other rondeaux here gathered is the reason of its insertion in the group.

For to love her repeats the ideas already met with : —

> " But she hath made another promess
> And hath given me leave full honestly.
>
> .   .   .   .
>
> Methink it best that readily
> I do return to my first address;
> For at this time *too great is the press,*
> *And perils appear too abundantly,*
> For to love her."

In connection with the last poem of this set, we must examine several others which have been mentioned in their respective places, but have not been as yet discussed. These productions, together with the rondeau remaining, may be looked upon as building a conclusion to the general thought of this large group, just as certain others united to serve as introductory to the whole. These poems are in all five.

	N.	A.
If it be so	150	27
Though this the port	157	61
O miserable sorrow	236	124
The joy so short	242	129
What death is worse	180	81

If it be so. The motive of the closing lines of this rondeau is to be found in Chaucer, who makes use of the image several times.

· In the "Booke of the Dutchesse," verse 1151, he says:

> "For wostou why? she was lady
> Of the body; she hadde the herte,
> And who hath that may not asterte."

In the "Romaunt of the Rose," too, we find, verse 2084 and following: —

> "For of the body he is full lord
> That hath the herte in his tresour."

In this poem the lover refers to a separation, — a separation which he regards as banishment. His heart remains true, and he is so far her devoted and obedient servant as to obey his lady's will even in departing from her presence, if she list so to order him. At the same time he has reason to suspect that her affection has changed; but comforts himself with the conceit that he still holds her heart in his possession, and therefore it is impossible for her to bestow it elsewhere.

Though this the port (Rhyme-royal Stanza).

> ". . . Behold yet how that I,
> *Banished from my bliss,* carefully do cry.
>
> . . . .
>
> By seas and hills elonged from my sight,
> Thy wonted grace reducing to my mind,
> Instead of sleep thus I occupy the night;
> A thousand thoughts, and many doubts I find,
> And still I trust thou canst not be unkind,
> Or else despair my comfort and my chere
> Would she forthwith, 'En vogant la Galere.' "

O! miserable sorrow (Rhyme-royal Stanza).

> "And this my last voice carry thou thither,
> Where lived my hope, now dead for ever:
> For as ill grievous *is my banishment,*
> As was my pleasure when she was present."

The joy so short (Rhyme-royal Stanza).

" The time doth pass, yet shall not my love ;
Though I be far, always my heart is near.
Though other change yet will not I remove;
Though other care not, yet love I will and fear;
Though other hate, yet will I love my dear;
Though other will of lightness say ' Adieu,'
Yet will I be found steadfast and true."

What death is worse : a b a b b a.

" What death is worse than this !
When my delight,
My weal, my joy, my bliss,
Is from my sight.

Heartless, alas ! what man   ·
May long endure !
Alas ! how live I then ;
Since no recure
May me assure
My life I may well ban."

This set of five poems evidently records a period of absence,
perhaps enjoined upon the lover by his lady. It would seem.
as if she sent him away with promises, and gladly availed herself of his absence to further her own designs. This episode
may be judged to fall at the close of the period which we have
been discussing, and helps to explain the sudden change which
now occurs in the sentiment of the compositions which follow.
Up to this point, it is remarkable that the lover still persists in
his hopeless attachment ; in every piece the assurance of his
constancy has been passionately affirmed : he now suddenly
casts off his bonds, and has recourse to taunts and upbraiding.
We are better prepared for the violent tone of the poems which
follow if we suppose the lover to have received this new proof
of his lady's heartlessness and insincerity. We here take up a
fourth group of Wyatt's productions, and leave what may be
called, perhaps, the period of Disappointment or Deception.

GROUP III. OF THE LOVE-POEMS.

SONNETS.	N.	T.	A.
I abide and abide . . .	144	—	20
Though I myself . . .	145	—	, 21
How oft have I . . .	13	69	14
Was I never yet . . .	2	33	2
RONDEAUX.			
Behold, Love! . . .	18	53	22
Go burning sighs! . . .	19	73	24
Help me to seek! . . .	147	—	24
For to love her . . .	148	—	25
If it be so . . .	150	—	27
SINGLE-RHYME.			
Forget not yet . . .	235	—	123
And wilt thou . . .	219	—	108
As power and wit . . .	221	—	111

abab STANZA.	N.	T.	A.
Disdain me not . . .	35	58	44
If Fancy would . . .	161	—	65
I have sought . . .	172	—	74
***abab* STANZA (SECOND SET).**			
Alas! poor man . . .	217	—	107
RHYME-ROYAL.			
It may be good . . .	28	42	37
That time that mirth . . .	220	—	109
Though this the port . . .	157	—	61
O miserable sorrow . . .	336	—	124
The joy so short . . .	243	—	139

ANOMALOUS.	N.	T.	A.
The knot which . . .	224	—	113
It was my choice . . .	226	—	114
Accused though I . . .	75	55	177
Perdie I said it . . .	40	66	48
Ye know my heart . . .	237	—	125
ANOMALOUS (SECOND SET).			
Though I cannot . . .	184	—	85
If with complaint . . .	237	—	125
The answer that . . .	38	62	46
Give place! all ye . . .	247	—	133
If chance assigned . . .	175	—	77
What death is . . .	180	—	81
Since Love will . . .	43	77	51
I see that chance . . .	46	81	53

GROUP IV.

a. *Sonnets.*

	N.	T.	A.
My love to scorn	10	55	11
My heart I gave	15	71	16
Divers doth use	143	—	20
To rail or jest	145	—	22
There was never file	2	34	2
Whoso list to hunt	143	—	19
Farewell, Love	17	70	18

My love to scorn.

"But since that thus ye list to order me,
That would have been your servant true and fast,
Displease thee not : my doting days be past.
And with my loss to leave I must agree.
For as there is a certain time to rage,
So is there time such madness to assuage."

My heart I gave.

" But, since it please thee to feign a default,
Farewell, I say, parting from the fire.
For he that believeth bearing in hand
Ploweth in the water, and soweth in the sand."

Divers doth use.

"And some there be that when it chanceth so
That women change, and hate where love hath been,
They call them false, and think with words to win
The hearts of them which otherwhere doth grow.
But as for me, though that by chance indeed
Change hath outworn the favour that I had,
I will not wail, lament, nor yet be sad,
Nor call her false that falsely did me feed ;
    But let it pass, and think it is of kind
That often change doth please a woman's mind."

To rail or jest.

> " Things of great weight I never thought to crave,
> This is but small; of right deny it not :
> Your feigning ways, as yet forget them not.
> But like reward let other lovers have ;
>> That is to say, for service true and fast,
>> Too long delays, and changing at the last."

There was never file.

> " But reason hath at my folly smiled,
> And pardoned me, since that I me repent
> Of my lost years, and time misspent.
> For youth did me lead, and falsehood guided."

Whoso list to hunt.

> " Whoso list to hunt ?   I know where is an hind !
> But as for me, alas ! I may no more,
> The vain travail hath wearied me so sore ;
> I am of them that furthest come behind.
>
> .   .   .   .
>
> Who list her hunt, I put him out of doubt
> As well as I, may spend his time in vain !
> And graven with diamonds in letters plain,
> There is written her fair neck round about ;
>> ' Noli me tangere ; *for Cæsar's I am*,
>> And wild for to hold, though I seem tame.' "

When read in the light of the other poems we have been
examining, there can be little doubt that the lady referred to
under the image of the " hind " is the lady whom the lover has
been pursuing all along.   The fact that she now bears mark of
Cæsar's ownership explains the ill-success of the former suitor,
and makes clear several allusions already noted.   This is, perhaps, the most convincing evidence we have regarding the identity of the poet's mistress.

Farewell, Love.

> " Farewell, Love, and all thy laws for ever;
> Thy baited hooks shall tangle me no more :

Senec, and Plato, call me from thy lore,
To perfect wealth, my wit for to endeavour.
.   .   .   .
Therefore, farewell ! go trouble younger hearts ;
And in me claim no more authority:
With idle youth go use thy property,
And thereon spend thy many brittle darts :   ·
    For, hitherto though I have lost all my time,
    Me lusteth no longer rotten boughs to climb."

Further comment seems unnecessary ; the poems speak sufficiently for themselves, and their similarity and relation are obvious.

b. *Rondeaux.*

	N.	T.	A.
What no, perdie !	149	—	26
What 'vaileth truth	18	53	23
Thou hast no faith	151	—	28
Ye old mule !	148	—	26

What no, perdie !

    " Too much it were still to endure.
    Truth is tried, where craft is in ure,
    But though ye have had my heartes cure,
    Trow ye I dote without ending ? "

What 'vaileth truth.

    " Soonest he speeds that most can feign ;
    True meaning heart is had in disdain.
    Against deceit and doubleness,
    What 'vaileth truth !
      Deceived is he by crafty train,
      That means no guile, and doth remain
      Within the trap, without redress :
      But for to love, lo, such a mistress,
      Whose cruelty nothing can refrain,
       What 'vaileth truth ! "

Thou hast no faith contains a taunt based upon the fickle character of his former mistress, who is now beloved of another.

This other suitor he characterizes as treacherous also, and quotes the proverb of "like to like."

> " I thought thee true without exception;
> But I perceive I lacked discretion,
> To fashion faith to words mutable.
> Thy thought is too light and variable,
> To change so oft without occasion.
> Thou hast no faith ! "

Ye old mule is bitterest of all Wyatt's pieces ; reflecting as it does upon the lady's sincerity of heart, and also applying to her an epithet used only of a woman of degraded character. The piece is expressive of the lover's feelings at this time, but is of such a nature as to make us doubtful whether we should assign it to this or to a later period, on the supposition that the allusion is quite different.

c. *Single-rhyme Stanza.*

	N.	T.	A.
Farewell the reign	28	44	36
Is it possible	216	—	106
Hate whom ye list	251	—	137

Farewell the reign.

> " Farewell the reign of cruelty !
> Though that with pain my liberty
> Dear have I bought, yet shall surety
> Conduct my thoughts of joy needy."

Is it possible.

> " It is possible
> For to turn so oft ;
> To bring that low'st that was most aloft ;
> And to fall highest, yet to light soft ;
> It is possible ! "

Hate whom ye list, which can hardly be called a poem, seems expressive of the sentiment of this period.

d. *Rhyme-royal Stanza.*

	N.	T.	A.
They flee from me	23	40	32
My hope alas	162	—	66
What should I say	246	—	132
Full well it may	228	—	117

They flee from me is interpreted by Dr. Nott in an allegorical sense throughout, and refers, according to his explanation, to Fortune thus personified. But the poem is suggestive of the sonnet *Whoso list to hunt?* (N. 143 ; A. 18) inasmuch as the poet begins with the figure of a deer, formerly tame, ready to take bread from his hand. There is no reason why we should doubt that a lady of flesh and blood is the one referred to here.

My hope, alas !

> " Sometime delight did tune my song,
> And led my heart full pleasantly;
> And to myself I said among —
> ' My hap is coming hastily.'
> But it hath happed contrary.
> Assurance causeth my distress,
> And I remain all comfortless."

What should I say.

> " I promised you,
> And you promised me,
> To be as true
> As I would be.
> But since I see
> Your double heart,
> Farewell my part ! "

Full well it may.

> " What thing may more declare
> Of love the crafty kind,
> Than see the wise so ware,
> In love to be so blind,
> ⸍ If so it be assigned;
> Let them enjoy the gain
> That thinks it worth the pain."

e. *a b a b Stanza.*

	N.	T.	A.
Where shall I have	26	51	35
If ever man	37	59	45
All heavy minds	164	—	67
Ah! Robin!	188	—	88
Since so ye please	233	—	121
Now must I learn	233	—	121

Where shall I have.

> " I speak not now to move your heart
> That you should *rue upon my pain;*
> The sentence given may not revert :
> I know such labour were but vain.
>
> .   .   .   .   .   .
>
> Fortune and you did me advance;
> Methought I swam, and could not drown :
> Happiest of all ; but my mischance
> Did lift me up, to throw me down.
>
> .   .   .   .   .   .
>
> Where are your pleasant words, alas ?
> Where is your faith ? your steadfastness ?
> There is no more but all doth pass,
> And I am left all comfortless."

Turning to the poem *Though I cannot your cruelty constrain* (N. 184 ; A. 85), we find the lover hopeless, but craving that his lady might *rue upon his pain.* That poem was conjectured to belong to the period preceding this of which we now speak. In verse 14 of the poem before us we may fairly judge that Wyatt has in mind a similar expression used on some former occasion, when he says he does not now speak to move his lady to be pitiful. The proverb " like to like," quoted in verse 24, has been already noted as applied in a different form in the rondeau *Thou hast no faith* (N. 151 ; A. 28). Further, the allusion to the fickleness of Fortune has been frequently met in the poems of this period.

8

It should be added that in the Harington MS. the following line is superscribed in Wyatt's hand : —

"*Podra ser che no es.*"

This leads Nott to suppose that the poem is translated from the Spanish, and probably written while Wyatt was in Spain. The piece may be an imitation ; but the phraseology and the thought are so often repetitions of what we find in other original poems that we must hesitate before we pronounce it a translation.

If ever man.

> "Sometime I stood so in her grace,
> That, as I would require,
> Each joy I thought did me' embrace,
> That furthered my desire.
>
> .   .   .   .   .   .
>
> For she hath turned so her wheel,
> That I, unhappy man,
> May wail the time that I did feel
> Wherewith she fed me than."

When we compare this with the two poems *Once as me-thought, Fortune me kissed* (N. 21 ; T. 63 ; A. 30) ; *After great storms the calm returns* (N. 156 ; A. 60), it is evident that *If ever man* is subsequent to those, and should be assigned to a later period; compared with *My hope, alas ! hath me abused* (N. 162 ; A. 66), the intimate connection is clearly seen : the two poems must go together.

All heavy minds.   '

> "I seek nothing
> But thus for to discharge
> My heart of sore sighing;
> To plain at large.
>   And with my lute
> Sometime to ease my pain ;
> For else all other suit
> Is clean in vain."

This poem introduces us to a set of "lute-songs," with which we shall soon become acquainted.

Ah ! Robin !

> " ' My lady is unkind, perdie ! '
> Alack, why is she so?
> ' She loveth another better than me,
> And yet she will say, No.' "

Since so ye please.

> " But cursed be that cruel heart
> Which hath procured a careless mind
> For me and my unfeignèd smart,
> And forceth me such faults to find."

Now must I learn.

> " I may no longer more endure
> My wonted life to lead ;
> But I must learn to put in ure
> The change of womanhed.
>
> .   .   .   .   .
>
> I ask none other remedy
> To recompense my wrong,
> But once to have the liberty
> That I have lacked so long."

f. *Anomalous.*

	N.	T.	A.
My lute awake	20	64	29
My pen ! take pain	207	—	98
At most mischief	177	—	78
Now all of change	256	—	141
Marvel no more	30	50	39
Alas the grief	168	—	71
If in the world	186	—	87
Since you will needs	239	—	127
How should I	243	—	130
Spite hath no power	249	—	135
Tangled I was	252	—	137

	N.	T.	A.
Blame not my lute	205	—	96
Patience for my device	181	—	82
Patience though I have not	182	—	83
Patience of all my smart	183	—	84
Patience for I have wrong	259	—	144
When first mine eyes	42	76	50

My lute awake : a a b a b.

> " My lute awake, perform the last
> Labour, that thou and I shall waste,
> And end that I have now begun :
> And when this song is sung and past,
> My lute ! be still, for I have done."

My pen, take pain : a a b a b.

> " My pen ! take pain a little space
> To follow that which doth me chase,
> And hath in hold my heart so sore ;
> But when thou hast this brought to pass,
> My pen ! I prithee write no more."

This poem is a close imitation of the preceding ; Nott calls it
" a parody," — a term hardly appropriate in this case.
At most mischief : a a a b c c c b.

> " At most mischief
> I suffer grief ;
> For of relief
> Since I have none,
> My lute and I
> Continually
> Shall us apply
> To sigh and moan."

Now all of change : a b c a b c.

> " Of Fortune's might
> That each compels,
> And me the most, it doth suffice ;
> Now for my right

To ask nought else
But to withdraw this enterprise.

. . . . . .

'   And she unjust
Which feareth not
In this her fame to be defiled,
Yet once I trust
Shall be my lot
To quite the craft that me beguiled."

Marvel no more : a b a b a c a c.

" Marvel no more although
The songs, I sing, do moan ;
For other life than woe,
I never proved none.
And in my heart also
Is graven with letters deep,
A thousand sighs and mo,
A flood of tears to weep."

The allusion in the closing stanza of this poem to a certain
Mistress Chaunce, or Souche, is not of great importance. There
was a Mistress Souche in existence at that time, whose portrait
by Holbein has come down to us, — possibly the reference is to
her ; and so Dr. Nott conjectures likely. If this be the case,
the introduction of the compliment here is a mere tribute of
gallantry to a beautiful woman.

Alas the grief : a a b a b b.

" I have wailed thus, weeping in nightly pain,
In sobs and sighs, alas ! and all in vain,
In inward plaint, and heart's woeful torment.
And yet, alas ! lo ! cruelty and disdain
Have set at nought a faithful true intent,
And price hath privilege truth to prevent."

If in the world : a b a a b c b d c e d e d.

" Who list to live in quietness
By me let him beware.

> For I by high disdain
> Am made without redress ;
> And unkindness, alas ! hath slain
> My poor true heart, all comfortless."

Since you will needs : a b a c b c.

> " A broken lute, untunèd strings,
> With such a song may well bear part,
> That neither pleaseth him that sings,
> Nor them that hear, but her alone
> That with her heart would strain my heart
> To hear it groan."

How should I : a a b c c b.

> " Whom I did trust,
> And think so just,
> *Another man hath won.*
>
> .   .   .   .
>
> Fortune did smile
> A right short while,
> And never said me nay ;
> With pleasant plays,
> And joyful days,
> My time to pass away.
> Where is the oath,
> Where is the troth,
> That she to me did give ?
> Such feignèd words
> With sely bourds
> Let no wise man believe."

Spite hath no power : a b a b b a b a.

> " Sometime my friend, farewell my foe,
> Since thou change I am not thine;
> But for relief of all my woe,
> It doth suffice that thou wert mine.
>   Praying you all that hear this song,
> To judge no wight, nor none to blame ;
> It doth suffice she doth me wrong,

And that herself doth know the same.
  And though she change it is no shame,
Their kind it is, and hath been long :
Yet I protest she hath no name ;
It doth suffice she doth me wrong."

Tangled I was : a a a b b b.

  " Too great desire was my guide,
  And wanton will went by my side,
  Hope ruled still and made me bide,
  Of Love's craft the extremity.
  But ha! ha! ha! full well is me,
  For I am now at liberty.
  With feignèd words, which were but wind,
  To long delays I was assigned ;
  Her wily looks my wits did blind.

    . . . . . .

  Was never bird tangled in lime
  That brake away in better time,
  Than I, that rotten boughs did climb,
  And had no hurt but scapèd free.
  Now ha! ha! ha! full well is me,
  For I am now at liberty."

The six poems which follow are all cast in one stanza form : a b a b c c.

Blame not my lute ! was evidently called forth by some complaint of the bitterness of his songs. Perhaps it follows with an interval, *My lute, awake* (N. 20 ; T. 64 ; A. 29).

  " Though my songs be somewhat strange,
    And speak such words as touch thy change,
      Blame not my Lute !

    . . . .

  Then though my songs be somewhat plain,
    And toucheth some that use to feign,
      Blame not my Lute !

    . . . . . .

And though the songs which I indite
Do quit thy change with rightful spite,
    Blame not my Lute !
.   .   .   .   .   .

Spite asketh spite, and changing, change,
And falsèd faith must needs be known ;
The faults so great, the case so strange ;
Of right it must abroad be blown :
Then since that by thine own desart
My songs do tell how true thou art,
    Blame not my Lute ! "

Patience for my device introduces to our notice a set of four poems, more or less closely related to each other. This first of the series represents a sarcastic dialogue between the discarded lover and his former mistress. The lover speaks in the opening stanza, saying : " I need patience on account of your treatment of me ; hence I adopt *patience* as my device. You, inasmuch as we are opposites by nature, shall take *impatience* for yours." The lady replies testily : " Patience ! yes ; and with good reason. You have no cause at all, and so, great need of patience ! " The rest of the dialogue is a rather obscure continuation of this counterplay of taunts and recrimination ; at the close the lady admits that she has accepted a new suitor. The word-play in the closing stanza springs from the last speech of the lover, who calls on the lady to have patience ; she rejoins : " The other (impatience) was for me ; this *patience* is for you."

The two following poems may be brought together thus :

Patience though I.	*Patience of all.*
" Patience ! though I have not	" Patience to have a nay,
The thing that I require ;	Of that I most desire ;
I must, of force, God wot,	Patience to have alway,
Forbear my most desire.	And ever burn like fire.
. . . . .	. . . . .
Was ever thought so moved,	For it doth well appear
To hate that it hath loved ?	My friend is turned my foe.
. . . . .	. . . . .

Patience of all my harm,
For Fortune is my foe;
Patience must be the charm
To heal me of my woe.
Patience without offence
Is a painful patience."

Patience of all my smart!
For Fortune is turned awry:
Patience must ease my heart,
That mourns continually.
Patience to suffer wrong
Is a patience too long."

Patience! for I have wrong.

"Patience! for I have wrong
And dare not shew wherein;
Patience shall be my song:
Since truth can nothing win."

When first mine eyes.

"When first mine eyes did view and mark
Thy fair beauty to behold;
And when my ears listened to hark
The pleasant words, that thou me told;
I would as then I had been free
From ears to hear, and eyes to see.
And when in mind I did consent
To follow this, my fancy's will,
And when my heart did first relent
To taste such bait, my life to spill;
I would my heart had been as thine,
Or else thy heart had been as mine."

g. *Ottava Rima.*

	N.	T.	A.
To wet your eye	210	—	101
Throughout the world	75	83	177
Desire, alas !	65	80	165
Sometime I fled	69	54	171

To wet your eye.

"Prate, and paint, and spare not,
Ye know I can me wreak;
And if so be ye can so not,
Be sure I do not reck;

And though ye swear it were not,
I can both swear and speak
By God, and by this cross
If I have the mock, ye shall have the loss."

Throughout the world.

"Throughout the world if it were sought,
Fair words enough a man shall find;
They be good cheap, they cost right nought,
Their substance is but only wind;
   But well to say and so to mean, —
   That sweet accord is seldom seen."

Desire, alas! is one of the most obscure of all Wyatt's poems. It is impossible to offer an explanation that shall be entirely to our satisfaction, but perhaps the best is this : —

"Desire, my master and my foe, how sorely altered mayst thou see thyself! Once thou didst seek her who is the cause of my uncertainty and despair; again thou didst inspire her with some degree of love, — the mistress who rules thee and me. What reason hast thou so to rule thy subjects? For where on thy account I expected to be blamed, so now, because of her hate, I fear it."

In the light of the poems discussed already, perhaps we may interpret as follows : Desire is the god of love. The lover addresses him, exclaiming over the fickleness of his rule. Now following, now leading, is the antithesis of verses 3, 4; the object of both the leading and the seeking is the lady loved. In the first case the lady is indifferent, and Desire must follow as a suitor; in the second case, Desire has imparted to the lady an affection for him who has been following, and so Desire is said to *lead* her who was the inspiration of the lover's passion. The closing couplet may refer to the peculiar circumstances of the lover's position. We saw in several poems that there was a degree of danger connected with the pushing of his suit, and that secrecy was necessary to safety. So here the lover doubted to have blame, while Desire, or Love, inspired his mistress to show him kindness and affection : this referring to that period designated by us as the period of Attainment. Now, the lover dreads the same because of his lady's hate.

> "Was ever thought so moved,
>   To hate that it hath loved?"
>
> N. 182; A. 83.

> "For it doth well appear
>   My friend is turned my foe."
>
> N. 183; A. 84.

> "Then in my book wrote my mistress
> 'I am yours, you may well be sure;
> And shall be while my life doth dure.'
>   But she herself which then wrote that
>   Is now mine extreme enemy.
>
>   .   .   .   .
>
> My love from her no man can let,
> Though never so sore they me threat."
>
> N. 220; A. 109.

This brings us to the period we have last been following, and it is to this period that the epigram probably belongs. The explanation is offered only in default of a better. The obscurity is too great to be easily penetrated; the confusion in the use of the word *desire* — at times employed to designate the god of love, at times referring to the passion of the lover or the affection of the lady — increases the difficulty of interpretation.

Sometime I fled is another exceedingly difficult poem. It has generally been interpreted as referring to the journey of Henry and Anne Boleyn to Calais in the year 1532 ; although in the list of those who accompanied them on that occasion, Wyatt's name is not found. There is quite an important variation in the reading of the two texts. The Harington MS. gives verses 4, 5 :

> "And now I follow the coals that be quent,
> From Dover to Calais, *against* my mind."

Where Tottel reads : —

> "And now, the coals I follow, that be quent,
> From Dover to Calais, with *willing* mind."

So in the last verse the MS. has : —

> "Meshed in the briars, that erst was, *all to torne*."

And Tottel : —

> ". . . that erst was *only* torn."

The MS. reading would seem to say : Once I fled to avoid the presence of this lady ; but it was sorely against my inclination. I am now compelled to follow in her train, and, strangely, find this nearness most distasteful. The last line of the epigram, inverted and involved after Wyatt's manner, should be read :

> "Who was first meshed in the briars, severely torn."

Tottel's reading is to be thus interpreted : I, who formerly sought by separation to overcome my affection for this lady, now follow willingly and unmoved in her company. I, who was then so blind, deceived; comprehend now, and am recovered. Then I acted as does one entangled in the briers, — struggled vainly to be free, when every effort bound me more closely.

In the absence of further evidence it is impossible to declare with certainty for either text. Neither reading affects the allusion, however, and so does not enter into the question of chronology. ˉ The date of the epigram is probably the year 1532, and the reference, that already indicated. This brings us to the end of our fourth period, — the period of Disillusion and Recovery.

We have now examined all the poems which appear to be intimately connected with Wyatt's own experiences during the years previous to 1532. Certain groups have been established, each consisting of a set of poems bound together by resemblances of style and form, as by similarity in thought and in expression. Little or no attempt has been made to arrange an order among the individual members of any set or group ; and the reader must remember that the arrangement by stanza form is one of convenience merely, the subordinate sets falling parallel with each other, not following, group by group, in the order in which they have necessarily been discussed. Whether *all* the poems gathered in any particular group really belong together, may easily be doubted by the student; and in many cases the writer has been equally in doubt. The possibility that Wyatt may have imitated pieces which pleased his fancy at a date later than that apparently indicated by their contents; the possibility, too, that we are at times interpreting into the poems the meanings we take out of them, — doubts like these make our task a by no means light one. But, granting that these hypotheses are not entirely unreasonable, there nevertheless remains enough of sincerity, enough of personality, to give a basis to our theory, and grounds for our conjectures.

The existence of these groups admitted, it is impossible not to recognize the order of their progress. There is a natural development which cannot be mistaken. The romance has sprung up of itself; there has been no artificial building: the materials were there, and have simply been placed in their right connection. There is nothing in it that conflicts with the record of Wyatt's life as it is known to us. The facts which we have noted are easily rehearsed. We saw in our sketch of the poet's life that he probably appeared at Court in 1520 or 1521. He was employed in various services, as we have seen, and sent with royal moneys to the North, in October and November of 1523. He participated in the feat of arms at Greenwich on Christmas Day of 1525, and in the following year spent the months of March, April, and May in France with Sir Thomas Cheney. In the early part of 1527 Wyatt visited Italy in company with Sir John Russell, and in 1528 took his position in the service at Calais. From 1524 to 1531 the poet held the office of Clerk of the King's Jewels. In 1532 he was made Commissioner of the Peace for Essex. These points are mentioned to show that Wyatt remained in public life, and, until his departure for Calais in 1528, was necessarily much at Henry's Court.

Among the most prominent of the maids of honor at that period was Anne Boleyn ; and with her name that of the poet has been associated from his own day to this. As to the real character of the relations existing between these two, there has been much conjecture. Dr. Nott devotes a deal of argument to proving the connection one of those platonic friendships which were common at the time, and were indeed the fashion, causing no great scandal or remark. While Nott admits the testimony of the poems as sufficient proof of this attachment, he has been severely ridiculed by other writers, who find no certain reference to Anne Boleyn in Wyatt's verses.

In the gossip of that day the names of Wyatt and Anne Boleyn were often coupled ; and whatever the cause of Wyatt's short imprisonment in 1536, it is evident from the letters we have read, that his fellow-courtiers, as a matter of course, referred it to the poet's old attachment for the queen. The poet's own grandson, George Wyatt, relates an anecdote to prove that the king and Wyatt were at one time rivals for the favor of the Lady Anne.[1] In regard to Wyatt's attachment, Dr. Nott has this to say : —

" Thus circumstanced, we may believe Wyatt and Anne Boleyn to have mutually regarded each other with the lively tenderness of an innocent, but a dangerous friendship. Often, I have no doubt, did Wyatt make her the subject of his most empassioned strains : and often did she listen with complacency to his numbers, which, while they gratified her love of present admiration, promised to con- fer upon her charms some portion of that poetic immortality which the romantic passion of Petrarch had bestowed on Laura's."[2]

To this we may add that Wyatt was a youth of not more than twenty years when he met Anne at Court, — herself a girl

---

[1] This anecdote is given entire in the biography prefixed to Wyatt's poems in the Aldine Edition, p. xv, quoted from the " Extracts from the Life of the Virtuous, Christian, and Renowned Queen Anne Boleigne. By George Wyatt, Esq.," p. 4.

[2] Nott's edition, Memoirs, p. xxi.

three years younger than the poet. In the biographical sketch contained in the Aldine Edition of Wyatt's poems (page xiv) the writer says : —

" It was about the year 1529 that Anne Boleyn also became con-nected with the Court as maid of honour to Queen Katharine."

But poor Queen Catharine was not in a position to need the services of new maids of honor in 1529 ; and Anne Boleyn had been a year or more the acknowledged mistress of the king when that year arrived. In regard to Anne's actual appearance at Henry's Court, Brewer says : —

" In the March of 1522 I find Mistress Anne Boleyn mentioned with other ladies as having charge of certain garments and dresses which had been used at a royal revel on the 4th of March in the same year; in other words, officially attached to the royal wardrobe." [1]

It is interesting to note that Anne had been already made the subject of laudatory verse even at that youthful age ; the writer of the verses being no less a poet than *Clément Marot*, the witty Frenchman. In this connection D'Héricault, the biographer of that poet, says : —

" C'est à la Cour de Marguerite, entre Clément Marot et Louis de Berquin, à cette fameuse escole d'amour et d'hérésie, qu' Ann de Boleyn apprit la haine de l'église romaine et cette science de galanterie à laquelle le pataud Henri VIII ne sut pas résister."

Referring to two important personages whom Marot met at the Court of Marguerite de Valois, one of whom was François Sagon, he says further : —

" L'autre, nous le trouvons au milieu de cette foule de demoi-selles d'honneur de Marguerite avec lesquelles le poëte gardera toujours des relations de courtoisie, quand il les retrouvera plus

---

[1] Calendar of State Papers, vol. iii., Int., p. 432.

tard à la cour de François 1ᵉʳ, et qu'il leur dédiera diverses pièces. Ce personnage n'est autre qu'Anne de Boleyn."[1]

Returning once more to our English poet, we may remark that it was very natural for Wyatt, with his head full of the poetry of Italy, and possibly that of France, — for it is ridiculous to assert that he was unacquainted with French and Italian literature previous to his visits abroad in 1526–27, — to cast his eye around for another Laura or Diane, to whom he might dedicate the verse he was beginning to translate and to compose. If his choice happened to fall upon the brilliant, fascinating Anne Boleyn — and what thing more likely ? — his verse would prove not at all unwelcome to this young coquette fresh from the Court of France, that school of gallantry and love, where she had already received the tribute offered by· the French poet to her charms. That Wyatt did make Anne Boleyn the subject of *some* poems has been pretty generally admitted ; the question still remains, Was she the heroine of all those compositions just examined by us ; and if so, was the poet really making love to her?

Wyatt was married, and had a son at the time he met Anne Boleyn. But Wyatt was a courtier, and at an age not noted for its prudence or its self-control. We have hardly space to discuss the character and reputation of Anne Boleyn ; she appears before us in as many different lights as there are historians to record her frailties and her misfortunes. The reader is referred to Brewer's admirable sketch of the queen, in the introduction to volume iv. of the Calendars. In one paragraph (page 244) he says : —

"Unquestionably after she became queen she permitted herself to be addressed by her inferiors with a freedom of language repugnant to the dignity of her sex ; and she even interchanged jests with them when they ventured to express their regard for her in terms more expressive of admiration than respect. Lively and attractive as she might be, she had not the qualities to inspire awe.

---

[1] *Œuvres de Clément Marot*, Paris, 1867, p. xliii.

In the estimation of those around her, she never at any time rose above the mistress; and her own equivocal position with the king lowered the whole moral tone of the circle in which she moved, and lent encouragement to laxity and licentiousness no English Court had witnessed before. How indeed could it be otherwise?"

Such was the character in part of the lady whom Wyatt had chosen "out of all the flock," if Anne is indeed the heroine of the love-songs. And the allusions and the circumstances all agree. The necessary secrecy; the impossibility of enjoying the love which apparently was mutual; the appearance of a rival suitor of higher rank; the warnings to his mistress to guard her honor against the tempting offers of position; the lament that he had loved above his poor degree; the determination to withdraw because another was in possession of the prize, and that it was Cæsar's mark that encircled the hind's fair neck,—seem to make the matter as evident as it could probably be safely made. The confession of the lady's name—"It is mine Anna, God it wot"—confirms the supposition of her identity, and leaves little doubt as to the fact. But these allusions here referred to occur in poems which are closely bound and interwoven with the rest. They are not apart from them, but they, together with them, form a whole. The subject of one is the subject of another: the reference may be clearer here than there; but the allusion is the same, and the one poem is to be interpreted in the light given by the other. As we progress in our study of the poet's work, we find that imitations cease; the compositions become personal and fervid: we find the record of real experiences and a real romance.

Beginning in 1522 or 1523, it reaches its turning-point about the year 1527, and its end in 1532. We say its turning-point in 1527; and here again, we have recourse to Brewer:—

"It is clear that he [Henry] felt piqued and uneasy at the attentions paid by others to Anne Boleyn, and endeavored to thwart them; but he had not yet discovered his intentions to himself, still less to others; and it is certain that he had only revealed them

9

partially to Wolsey. . . . It was not until 1525 that Wolsey became aware of the real state of the king's mind.[1] . . . The whole affair was carried on with profound secrecy, . . . nor does the name of Anne Boleyn ever occur. In 1527 it was buzzed about in every ear, and every tongue was talking about it." [2]

It is therefore evident that the crisis was reached some time before that date, which is retained as giving a convenient point of division in setting limits to the different periods of Wyatt's activity.

As to the success of this love-affair, we may judge from the allusions in the poems that Wyatt won, or thought he had won, the affection of the lady. But this period of happiness was very short, and it may well be doubted from the evidence of the other poems that Anne ever bestowed her heart upon the poet at all. Probably she coquetted with his affection for a time, and then discarded him altogether, as the king's attachment claimed her notice. One thing is pretty certain, — at least as certain as anything in this connection ·can be, — and that is, that no un-lawful intercourse ever stained their friendship. In the poem *Mine old dear en'my* (N. 50 ; T. 40 ; A. 149), a piece which gives probably a comprehensive sketch of this whole episode, Wyatt protests, with evident sincerity, speaking in the person of the god of love (verse 115), —

> "That by my means in no manner of wise
> Never vile pleasure him hath overthrown."

From the strain in which the poet speaks in this production, we judge it written subsequent to the marriage, and previous to the downfall, of the queen, — that is, between the years 1533 and 1536.

We have now to consider briefly the remaining productions of Wyatt's pen. These may be arranged in two more groups, — a fifth group of love-songs, and a final set of later poems of a slightly different character.

---

[1] Calendar of State Papers, vol. iv., Int., p. 246.   [2] Ibid., p. 252.

GROUP IV. OF THE LOVE-POEMS.

SONNETS.	N.	T.	A.
My love to scorn.	10	55	11
My heart I gave.	15	71	16
Divers doth use.	143	—	20
To rail or jest.	145	—	22
There was never file	2	34	2
Whoso list to hunt	143	—	19
Farewell, Love	17	70	18
RONDEAUX.			
What no, perdie!	149	—	26
What 'vaileth truth	18	53	23
Thou hast no faith	151	—	28
Ye old mule!	148	—	26
OTTAVA RIMA.			
To wet your eye.	210	—	101
Throughout the world	75	83	177
Desire, alas!	65	80	165
Sometime I fled	69	54	171

SINGLE-RHYME.	N.	T.	A.
Farewell the reign	28	44	36
Is it possible	216	—	106
Hate whom ye list	251	—	137
RHYME-ROYAL.			
They flee from me	23	40	32
My hope alas	162	—	66
What should I say	246	—	132
Full well it may	228	—	117
***a b a b* STANZA.**			
Where shall I have	26	51	35
If ever man	37	59	45
All heavy minds	164	—	67
Ah! Robin!	188	—	88
Since so ye please	233	—	121
Now must I learn	233	—	121

ANOMALOUS.	N.	T.	A.
My lute awake	20	64	29
My pen I take pain	207	—	98
At most mischief	177	—	78
Now all of change	256	—	141
Marvel no more	30	50	39
Alas the grief	163	—	71
If in the world	186	—	87
Since you will	239	—	127
How should I	243	—	130
Spite hath no	249	—	135
Tangled I was	252	—	137
Blame not my	205	—	96
Patience for my	181	—	82
Patience though I	182	—	83
Patience of all	183	—	84
Patience for I	259	—	144
When first mine	42	76	50

GROUP V.

a. *Sonnets.*

	N.	T.	A.
You ! that in love	5	36	5
If waker care	6	36	6

b. *Single-rhyme Stanza.*

In æternum	189	—	89
Ah ! my heart	250	—	136
A lady gave me	80	223	183

c. *Rhyme-royal Stanza.*

In faith I wot not	29	44	38
And if an eye	159	—	63
Mine old dear en'my	50	46	149

d. *a b a b Stanza.*

There was never	153	—	57
Will ye see	259	—	144
Madam, withouten	76	41	178

e. *Ottava Rima.*

A face that should	64	68	164
From these high hills	68	46	169
It burneth yet, alas !	78	79	180
It is a grievous smart	212	—	103
Of Carthage, he	71	83	173
Tagus, farewell	71	84	173

f. *Anomalous.*

Your looks so often	33	57	41
O goodly hand	158	—	62
Lo ! what it is	191	—	90
Leave thus to slander	192	—	92
Since love is such	230	—	118
Deem as ye list	261	—	145
Me list no more	240	—	128
So feeble is the thread	56	73	154

There is one prominent characteristic, common to all the poems here collected, which, more than anything else, separates and distinguishes them from those that have preceded. In all the compositions hitherto discussed there is a strong personal element, which stamps upon each production of that time the impression of a definite purpose and a specific address. In these, upon the contrary, this definiteness, this manifest directness, is almost entirely wanting. The poet, to be sure, sings of love and passion yet; but there is a generalness and an indefiniteness in every piece. This will be more clearly seen by an examination of the poems individually. Add to this pervasive characteristic other qualities, such as the deepening in sentiment, the increased facility of expression, the freedom from the turbulence of the earlier productions, — and these are the reasons for gathering the poems named in a common group.

You ! that in love (class *a*). This sonnet was apparently intended to record some accident of fortune occurring in the month of May. It has generally been referred to the events of May, 1536, — the period of Anne Boleyn's disgrace and of Wyatt's own imprisonment and accusation. In our preliminary sketch of the poet's life it was noted that in May of 1535 Wyatt underwent an earlier imprisonment; and this fact may give greater force to the expression, —

> "That me betide in May most commonly."

There is no reason why we should not accept the general tradition, and assign the poem to the year 1536, or soon thereafter.

There are several suggestions of Chaucer in this sonnet, for in that writer we find the following : —

> "Do wey your book, ryse up, and let us daunce,
> And lat us do to May som observaunce."
>
> T. and C. ii. 111.

> "Now thanketh God, he may gone in the daunce
> Of him that Love liste fiebly for tavaunce."
>
> T. and C. i. 517.

And for al that was he sete behynde
With hem that Love liste fiebly to avaunce."
Comp. of Blk. K. 353.

" For ye that reigne in youth and lustynesse."
Court of Love, 176.

"And freshe Beaute Lust and Jolyte."
Comp. to Pitie, 39.

If waker care evidently belongs to a period when Wyatt's art was well developed. The motive is the discovery of second love in the poet's breast. Phyllis now claims the affection formerly bestowed on Brunet, — a name appropriately referred to the unhappy queen, who had "set his wealth in such a roar," or as the line originally read : —

" Her that did set our country in a roar."

" The alteration, which is in Wyatt's own hand, was made probably that the person intended might not appear too closely designated." [1] The date of the poem must be somewhat later than that of the preceding. It would be pleasant to refer the Phyllis of the sonnet to the poet's wife; but it is probably to be taken merely as a compliment of gallantry to some lady of the circle in which the poet moved.

In æternum (class *b*) is a poem similar in character to that just examined.

" In æternum then from my heart I cest
That, I had first determined for the best;
Now in the place *another* thought doth rest
In æternum."

Ah ! my heart.

" Thou know'st full well that but of late,
I was turned out of Love's gate :
And now to guide me to this mate !
Ah! my heart, what aileth thee ? "

A lady gave me may be assigned, perhaps, to this period.

[1] Nott, Notes, p. 539.

In faith I wot not (class *c*) seems to be an expression of re-
joicing over the outcome of events in June, 1536. From allusions in Wyatt's speech in his defence, one may gather that the
accusations, of whatever kind they were, which led to his imprisonment at that time, were the result of a conspiracy among
some who were envious at his rapid advance and the general
favor with which he was regarded by the king and his own
associates. Wyatt himself said in his defence before the Privy
Council that his imprisonment was due to the enmity of the
Duke of Suffolk, not to the ill-will of Henry. If such were the
case, very likely these private enemies resorted to the old stories
of Wyatt's relations with Anne Boleyn to bring the poet under
suspicion at this dangerous time. Interpreting in the light of
these surmises, we should see considerable force in the allusions
of the second stanza to his innocence of the alleged offence, and
in the closing verses to the discomfiture of his enemies on his
acquittal, and immediate promotion to a command in the army
under the Duke of Norfolk. We can hardly reconcile the allusions made to the circumstances of his love-affair; and therefore
the piece is placed in this later group, and assigned to the
month of June or July of 1536.

And if an eye may possibly belong to an earlier period; but
the earnest, dignified style is more in harmony with the present.
The situation may as easily be an artificial as a real one. The
motive is this. A lover becomes suspicious of his lady's good
faith. He has seen her in a public place bestow a glance "all
soul" upon a possible rival. This he charges on the lady, who
becomes indignant, and retorts that he is blinded by his jealousy·
The lover now speaks in the words of the poem before us. He
wishes to conciliate, and is willing to let the matter pass as acci-
dental. Still he cannot but think the lady's heart was revealed
in the glance vouchsafed, and that what belongs of right to him
should be bestowed on him alone, not dispensed for all men's
pleasure indiscriminately. He shows her that the charge of
jealousy is unfair; for by her own admission she has testified

that others besides himself have thought the same. He now leaves further discussion, urging the lady to keep to Truth, and cherish that; then there will be no danger of misunderstanding or suspicion. If the poem falls more appropriately under an earlier date, it is to be placed in the group with the sonnet *Though I myself* (N. 145; A. 21).

There was never (class *d*) is too simple and unaffected to be the work of an earlier period. It is tender enough to be the record of a real experience.

Will ye see. It may be said that this poem is exactly in the style of those assigned to the earliest period; but there is an important difference. The sentiment is the same, and there is much of the like excess of imagery; but when we compare this piece with, for instance, *Like as the wind* (N. 81; A. 184), a poem similar in many points to this, we feel a difference, although it may not easily be defined.

In the composition now before us Wyatt introduces two quite new comparisons, — the rock of magnet, and the phœnix. This is the first time we have met them in his poetry. Judging, however, from the continual recurrence of a favorite image, even of expressions and phrases pleasing to his fancy, is it not probable that Wyatt would have served us these two striking figures in a variety of ways if he had come upon them sooner? The thought in the fifth stanza of *Like as the wind* is just the contrary of that expressed in the allusion to the phœnix. In the former —

> " I feel and see my own decay,
>   As one that beareth flame in his breast;"

in the poem now under discussion —

> " The flame whereof doth aye repair
>   My life when it is gone."

A similar thought is introduced again in *At last withdraw your cruelty* (N. 209; A. 100). But the "renewal" is there brought about by a flood of stormy tears, which averts the danger of martyrdom by fire, but exposes to peril of death by drowning.

The flames then burst forth once more, and the process is repeated; and so the lover alternates in a dreary way between the deaths which never come to his relief. Very different is the treatment of this idea of a deathly pain ever renewed, which we find in *Will ye see.*

Madam withouten is evidently a mere exercise of fancy.

A face that should (class *e*). This beautiful little poem is certainly a late work. Everything points to this assumption. It is not addressed to any new-found mistress, but is simply a pretty picture, perhaps suggested by the lingering memory of some fair one by whose lovely face the poet had been charmed. Some attempt has been made to refer the poem to a remark of Wyatt's quoted by his grandson in the work already mentioned (compare Aldine Edition, page xv). But Anne's personal appearance was quite other than that here described.

" From her Irish descent she inherited

'The black-blue Irish hair and Irish eyes.'

She was a little lively, sparkling brunette, with fascinating eyes and long black hair, which, contrary to the sombre fashion of those days, she wore coquettishly floating loosely down her back, interlaced with jewels." [1]

However well the rest of Wyatt's drawing may correspond with the original of this description, there is certainly no resemblance in the tress of " crisped gold." In his *Complaint of the Absence of his Love*, the poet refers to one of the charms of the lady whose absence he laments as " the crisped gold that doth surmount Apollo's pride " (verse 69). As Nott points out in his notes to the poem we are now considering (page 554), golden hair was the favorite type with the earlier poets. Compare Chaucer in his *Court of Love*, verse 138 : —

> " And all her here it shone as gold so fyne
> Disshivill, crispe, downe hyngyng at her bak
> A yarde in length."

[1] Brewer, Introduction to vol. iv. of the Calendars, p. 236.

In .the closing verse of the epigram Wyatt returns to his favorite metaphor, the "knot that should not slide." It is this verse which leads the editor of the Aldine edition to connect the poem with the allusion in George Wyatt's remark.

From these high hills may have been written while Wyatt was among the mountain-scenery of Spain. It is evidently a mature production, written after the experiences of his early passion had become a memory of the past.

It burneth yet, alas ! is indeed a love-poem; but it is an artificial situation, it is not a love-letter. In spite of the warm and passionate nature of the motive, the piece itself is cool and decorous.

It is a grievous smart is possibly a companion-piece to the above; it might well be. In this poem Wyatt gives us the pitiful picture of a woman betrayed by her lover, lamenting the consequences of her folly. The form of stanza followed would properly bring this composition under the class of anomalous forms, which follows; it adopts ·the rhyme-order *a b a b c c.*

Of Carthage, he, and *Tagus, farewell,* are plainly designated as composed in Spain. The former was written probably in the year 1538, as Wyatt declares —

> " At Mountzon thus I restless rest in Spain."

The *Farewell* was composed in 1539 as the poet was leaving Spain for England.

Your looks so often (class *f*) forms a pendant to *Take heed by time* (N. 208 ; A. 99). It follows the arrangement *a b a b b c b c.*

O goodly hand is to be reckoned similar to *There was never nothing* (N. 153 ; A. 57), *A face that should* (N. 64 ; T. 68 ; A. 164), etc. The arrangement followed is *a a b c c b.*

Lo ! what it is and *Leave thus to slander* belong together. The second poem is a rejoinder to the first, — a double reply, in fact. The first section replies in corresponding stanzas to each charge made in the preceding poem ; the second part is an attack upon the one who made the charges. The rhyme-order is the same in both, — *a a b b a b b a.*

Since love is such is a poetical confession of early folly. " For in my years of reckless youth " must not be taken as indicating any very long interval between the past and present ; in the last stanza the poet refers to the " power of Love *so late* out-cast." The thought with which he closes is this : Love was, not long ago, expelled ; but his power still rules in my breast, through the force of a *new* love which now possesses me. It would be pleasant if we might connect this new love, occa-sionally alluded to, with the legitimate object of the poet's attachment, — his wife. But probably no serious passion is alluded to. Rhyme-order, *a b a b b a b a.*

Deem as ye list is similar to *And if an eye* (N. 159 ; A. 63), the sentiment of which it seems to continue. It may have been intended for singing ; the burden was adopted in the song entitled *No foe to a flatterer,* in the *Paradise of Dainty Devices* (Nott, Notes, p. 586). The stanza-form is *a b a b c a c b.*

Me list no more — a a a b b — may be assigned to this period as appropriately as to any. The poet ends his puzzling oracular remarks with a sarcastic laugh at his perplexed auditors : —

> " For I reck not a bean ;
> I wot what I do mean ! "

So feeble is the thread. This fine poem, composed in couplets of twelve and fourteen syllable lines alternating, forming what is commonly designated " poulter's measure," is superscribed in the Harington MS. with the words " In Spain," written in Wyatt's own handwriting. It belongs then to the year 1538 or 1539, — probably to the former.

This brings us to the end of our fifth period, — that of the later love-poems

Group VI.

We now reach the sixth and final period of Wyatt's work, —
the period subsequent to the year 1539. The following compositions may be assigned to this group : —

a. *Sonnets.*

	N.	T.	A.
The pillar perished is	16	72	18
The flaming sighs	15	71	17

b. *Rhyme-royal Stanza.*

Right true it is	68	42	169
Driven by desire.	76	84	178
In Court to serve	74	83	176
If thou wilt mighty be	48	224	55

c. *a b a b Stanza.*

Most wretched heart	196	—	95

d. *Ottava Rima.*

Mistrustful minds	80	78	182
Sighs are my food	72	82	174
Look, my fair falcon	72	68	174
He is not dead	73	54	175
Venemous thorns	73	223	175
In doubtful breast	66	84	166

e. *Anomalous Forms.*

Stand whoso list.	74	83	176
Within my breast	77	56	179
Speak thou and speed	81	224	184
When Dido feasted first . . .	60	93	159
The Three Satires	82	85	186

The Paraphrase of the Seven Penitential Psalms.

The pillar perished is (class *a*) ; This sonnet is imitated from Petrarch's *Rotta è l'alta Colonna.* It was written on the occasion of the death of Cromwell, the powerful minister whose friendship, as we have seen, had been such a factor in Wyatt's history. The event took place in July, 1540.

The flaming sighs belongs to the period of Wyatt's last imprisonment. This began about the beginning of the year 1541, and continued until July of that same year.

Right true it is (class *b*) and *Driven by desire* probably allude to one event ; the two epigrams may belong to the period of imprisonment, like the preceding, or they may be assigned to a slightly later date.

In Court to serve is to be referred to the period of quiet retirement at Allington, lasting from July, 1541, until October, 1542. This short poem is suggestive of the Satires, and evidently belongs to the same period with them.

If thou wilt mighty be is commonly interpreted as alluding to the king. Its tone and subject force us to add it to the group.

Most wretched heart (class *c*) is not a love-poem. It, too, belongs to the period of confinement and of trial. It represents a dialogue between the sufferer and Despair.

> " And he that knoweth what is what,
> Saith he is wretched that weens him so,"

may be referred to Chaucer, who utters this thought in verse 25 of the *Ballade de Vilage Sauns Peynture :*

> " No man is wrechched but himself yt wene,
> And he that hath himself hat suffisaunce."

Mistrustful minds (class *d*), *Sighs are my food,* and *Look ! my fair falcon,* all belong to the prison period. The second of the three is addressed to one of Wyatt's intimate friends, Sir Francis Bryan.

He is not dead probably belongs to the same period of imprisonment ; as does the next epigram, *Venemous thorns.*

In doubtful breast may be best assigned to the latest division of Wyatt's work. An incident related by Josephus suggested the poem, which is unlike anything else that Wyatt has done. It passes more fitly with the productions of these last years than among the love-poems of an earlier time.

Stand whoso list (class *e*) is a companion-piece to *In Court to serve*, and belongs to the quiet days at Allington, just before the poet's death.

Within my breast is a poem of the same character and date ; and this may be said also of the following epigram, *Speak thou and speed.* All three of these short compositions are very suggestive of passages in Wyatt's Satires, and are closely connected with them in date of production.

When Dido feasted first, like *So feeble is the thread,* is composed of alternate hexameters and septenars. The piece is but a fragment, possibly left unfinished because of the advent of the new system of Copernicus, possibly because the poet's labors were interrupted midway by death. The fragment itself is very carefully wrought out and finished. It may have been begun in Spain in 1538 or 39, as it reads somewhat like a translation, and in the Spanish, of all literatures, might such a work be found. In the absence of evidence, however, it has seemed best to refer the poem to the later date, — the last few months of Wyatt's life.

The date of composition for the three Satires is fixed by allusions contained in them ; notably in the Second Satire :

v. 80. "This maketh me at home to hunt and hawk."

v. 89. " I am not now in France, to judge the wine ;
    With savory sauce the delicates to feel :
    Nor yet in Spain, where one must him incline
    Rather than to be, outwardly to seem.
    I meddle not with wits that be so fine ;
    Nor Flander's cheer lets not my sight to deem
    Of black and white ; nor takes my wit away
    With beastliness ; such do those beasts esteem.

Nor I am not, where Christ is given in prey,
For money, poison and trahison ; at Rome
A common practice, used night and day.
But here I am in Kent and Christendom,
Among the muses, where I read and rhyme,
Where if thou list, my Poins, for to come,
Thou shalt be judge, how I do spend my time."

These were among the last productions of Wyatt's pen ;
they reflect throughout the ripeness of his experience and the
skill and mastery he had attained. The Satires, indeed, may
be regarded as the most successful of his compositions, and as
that portion of his work most deserving to endure.

This same period of the life at Allington was devoted finally
to the composition of Wyatt's most ambitious work, the Paraphrase of the Seven Penitential Psalms. The reasons for and
the significance of that work have been sufficiently discussed
in the preliminary sketch of Wyatt's life. The Psalms themselves are composed in the same metre as the Satires ; the
arrangement of the verses in both is that known as the *terzine,*
the rhymes following the scheme *a b a, b c b, c d c,* etc.
These are the only ones among Wyatt's compositions in which
this order is adopted. Each Psalm is introduced by a prologue
from the author's pen. The prologues are cast in the *ottava-
rima* stanza, like most of the epigrams. Of the Paraphrase
as a whole it must be said that it is among the least successful
of Wyatt's efforts. The style is heavy and tedious ; the versification often rough and faulty.

CONCLUSION.

W E have now completed our survey of Wyatt's work. Our examination of the poems primarily for the purpose of gleaning new facts in regard to the poet's life has resulted in a grouping of his productions chronologically arranged. These groups may be thus stated.

> Group of Earliest poems . . . . . previous to 1522
> Group   I. Of the Love-poems . . . . . ⎫
>   „   II.   „   „   „   . . . . . ⎬ 1522–27
>   „   III.   „   „   „   1527–32
>   „   IV.   „   „   „   1532–36
>   „   V. Occasional poems 1536–39
>   „   VI. Late poems˙ 1539–42

The second group is comparatively small, and to attempt to limit the extent of Group I. would be so unsatisfactory that it is left thus undecided. It will be noted that the double period 1532–39 contains the fewest compositions ; it was at this time, if at any, that Wyatt made those alterations in his early poems which we find incorporated in Tottel's Miscellany.

A tabular view of Wyatt's poems, systematically and chronologically arranged, is for convenience appended.

YAL.	N.	T.	A	OTTAVA RIMA.	N.	T.	A.	ANOMALOUS.	N.	T.	A.
·m me,	23	40	3?	To wet your eye,	210	—	101	My lute awake,	20	64	29
s ?	1??	—	66	Throughout the,	75	83	177	My pen I take,	207	—	98
?,	246	—	13?	Desire, alas!	65	80	165	At most mischief,	177	—	78
?ay,	2?8	—	117	Sometime I fled,	69	54	171	Now all of change,	256	—	141
								Marvel no more,	30	50	39
								Alas the grief,	168	—	71
								If in the world,	186	—	87
								Since you will,	239	—	127
								How should I,	243	—	137
								Spite hath no,	249	—	135
								Tangled I was,	252	—	137
								Blame not my,	205	—	96
								Patience for my,	181	—	82
								Patience though I,	182	—	83
								Patience of all,	183	—	84
								Patience for I,	259	—	144
								When first mine,	42	76	50
?t,	29	44	38	A face that should,	64	68	164	Your looks so,	33	57	41
?e,	199	—	63	From these high,	68	46	169	O goodly hand,	158	—	62
?r,	50	40	149	It burneth yet,	78	79	180	Lo! what it is,	191	—	90
				It is a grievous,	212	—	103	Leave thus to,	192	—	92
				Of Carthage, he,	71	83	173	Since love is,	230	—	118
				Tagus, farewell,	71	84	173	Deem as ye,	261	—	145
								Me list no,	240	—	118
								So feeble is,	56	73	154
is,	68	42	169	Mistrustful minds,	80	78	182	Stand whoso list,	74	83	176
?sire,	76	84	178	Sighs are my food,	72	82	174	Within my breast,	77	56	179
?erve,	74	83	176	Look, my fair falcon,	72	68	174	Speak thou and,	81	224	184
	48	224	55	He is not dead,	73	54	175	When Dido feasted,	60	93	159
				Venemous thorns,	73	223	175	Three Satires, ∨	82	85	186
				In doubtful breast,	66	84	166	The Psalms.			

EARLIEST POEMS. **PREVIOUS TO 1522.**	Avising the bright,	10	40	11						
	Ever mine hap,	12	68	13						
	Love and Fortune,	12	69	13						
	Like to these,	13	70	15						

	The long love,	1	33	1
	The lively sparks,	3	34	3
	Such vain thought,	4	35	4
GROUP I.	Unstable dream,	4	35	4
PERIOD OF ENTREATY.	[Cæsar when that,	6	37	6]
	[Each man tells,	7	37	7]
1522-	Some fowls there,	7	38	8
	Because I have,	8	38	8
	I find no peace,	9	39	9
	My galley charged,	9	39	10
	Such is the course	11	68	12
	If amorous faith,	14	70	15

GROUP II.

PERIOD OF ATTAINMENT.

-1527.

	I abide and abide,	144	—	20	Behold,	I	18	53	22
	Though I myself,	145	—	21	Go burn	ghs	17	73	24
GROUP III.	How oft have I,	13	69	14	Help me	eek	147	—	24
	Was I never yet,	11	33	2	For to lo	er,	148	—	25
ERIOD OF DISAPPOINTMENT.					If it be s		150	—	27

1527-32.

E-RHYME.	N.	T.	A.	CROSS-RHYME.	N.	T.	A.	RHYME-ROYAL.	N.	T.	A.	OTTAVA RIMA.	N.	T.	A.	ANOMALOUS.	N.	T.	A
				Absence absenting, 258	—		142	Like as the wind, 47		105	54	For shamefast,	65	82	165				
												Vulcan begat,	65	82	166				
neaneth,	215	—	105	So unwarely,	37	65	47	Thou rentest place, 24	45		33	The furious gun,	70	54	171	My love is like,	232	—	120
se accord,	173	—	80	Comfort thyself,	166	—	70	Resound my voice, 25	43		34					At last withdraw,	209	—	100
h and,	173	—	75	Heaven and,	154	—	58	For want of all, 76	57		44					Heart oppressed,	207	—	116
age is this.	45	80	52	Process of time,	185	—	86	What would that, 83	223		183					Love doth again,	253	—	130
				Like as the swan,	187	—	87									Since ye delight,	169	—	72
				Like as the wind,	—	—	184									Sufficed not,	78	76	180
																Lo how I seek,	231	—	119
																Pass forth my,	32	56	40
eed by time, 208	—		99	Once as me thought, 21	63		30					The fruit of all,	276	—	174	Such hap as I,	171	—	73
se I sigh,	273	—	112	After great storms, 196	—		60					Of purpose Love,	64	83	164	To seek each,	159	—	56
I am,	292	—	147	I love, loved,	211	—	102					Alas! Madam,	66	41	167				
				The heart and,	214	—	104					The wand'ring,	67	41	167				
												What needeth,	67	42	168				
												She sat and,	69	31	170				
												Who hath heard,	69	52	170				
												Picture that gave,	70	65	177				
												All in thy look,	71	66	172				
												Th' enemy of,	67	63	168				
not yet,	215	—	173	Disdain me not,	35	58	43	It may be good, 28	42		30					The knot which,	224	—	113
It thou,	219	—	108	If Fancy would,	161	—	65	That time that, 221	—		107					It was my,	206	—	114
er and,	221	—	111	I have sought,	172	—	74	Though this the, 157	—		62					Accused though,	75	55	177
				Alas! poor man,	217	—	107	O miserable, 221	—		109					Perdie I said,	40	66	48
								The joy so short, 247	—		129					Ye know my,	237	—	175
																Though I cannot,	184	—	85
																If with complaint,	237	—	125
																The answer that,	38	60	46
																Give place I all ye, 247	—	133
																If chance assigned, 175	—	77
																What death is,	180	—	81
																Since Love will,	43	77	51
																I see that chance,	46	81	53

THE POEMS OF SIR THOMAS WYATT SYSTEMATI

	SONNETS.	N.	T.	A.	RONDEAUX.	N.	T.	A.	SINGLE-RHYME.	N.
GROUP IV. PERIOD OF RECOVERY. 1532–36.	My love to scorn, My heart I gave, Divers doth use, To rail or jest, There was never file, Whoso list to hunt, Farewell, Love,	10 15 143 145 2 143 17	55 71 — — 34 — 70	11 16 20 22 2 19 18	What no, perdie ! What 'vaileth truth, Thou hast no faith, Ye old mule !	149 18 151 148	— 53 — —	26 23 28 26	Farewell the reign, Is it poss ble, Hate whom ye,	18 216 251
GROUP V. OCCASIONAL POEMS. 1536–39.	You I that in love, If waker care,	5 6	36 36	5 6					In æternum, Ah ! my heart, A lady gave me,	1 2
GROUP VI. LATE POEMS. 1539–42.	The pillar perished, The flaming sighs,	16 15	72 71	18 17						

A.	CROSS-RHYME.	N.	T.	A.	RHYME-ROYAL.	N.	T.	A.	OTTAVA RIMA.	N.	T.	A.	ANOMALOUS.	N.	T.	A.
36	Where shall I have,	26	51	35	They flee from me,	23	40	30	To wet your eye,	110	—	101	My lute awake,	20	64	29
106	If ever man,	37	50	45	My hope alas !	112	—	66	Throughout the,	75	83	177	My pen I take,	207	—	98
137	All heavy minds,	164	—	67	What should I,	146	—	132	Desire, alas !	65	80	165	Now all of change,	296	—	141
	Ah ! Robin !	188	—	88	Full well it may,	208	—	117	Sometime I fled,	69	54	171	Marvel no more,	30	90	39
	Since so ye please,	133	—	121									Alas the grief,	168	—	71
	Now must I learn,	233	—	171									If in the world,	186	—	67
													Since you will,	239	—	177
													How should I,	243	—	131
													Spite hath no,	249	—	135
													Tangled I was,	250	—	137
													Blame not my,	205	—	96
													Patience for my,	181	—	81
													Patience though I,	182	—	83
													Patience of all,	183	—	84
													Patience for I,	239	—	144
													When first mine,	42	76	50
89	There was never,	151	—	57	In faith I wot,	99	44	98	A face that should,	64	68	164	Your looks so,	33	57	42
176	Will ye see,	239	—	144	And if an eye,	150	—	63	From these high,	68	76	169	O goodly hand,	158	—	61
183	Madam withouten,	76	41	178	Mine old dear,	50	40	149	It burneth yet,	78	79	180	Lo ! what it is,	191	—	90
									It is a grievous,	212	—	103	Leave thus to,	192	—	92
									Of Carthage, he,	71	83	173	Since love it,	230	—	118
									Tagus, farewell,	71	84	173	Deem as ye,	261	—	145
													Me list no,	240	—	128
													So feeble is,	56	73	154
	Most wretched heart,	196	—	95	Right true it is,	68	42	169	Mistrustful minds,	80	78	282	Stand whoso list,	74	83	176
					Driven by desire,	76	84	178	Sighs are my food,	72	82	174	Within my breast,	77	56	179
					In Court to serve,	74	83	176	Look, my fair falcon,	70	68	174	When Dido feasted,	60	93	159
					If thou wilt,	48	224	55	He is not dead,	73	54	175	Three Satires, V	82	85	186
									Venemous thorns,	73	223	175	The Psalms.			
									In doubtful breast,	66	84	166				

A REGISTER OF THE POEMS.

———•———

INDEX.